AF743433

The Library | UNIVERSITY OF BATH

Bath BA2 7AY · United Kingdom

10.00 a.m. 2 1 MA

16

Singular and Different

Singular and Different

Business in China
Past, Present and Future

Ian Rae

and

Morgen Witzel

palgrave
macmillan

© Ian Rae and Morgen Witzel 2004

All rights reserved. No reproduction, copy or transmission of this publication may be made without written permission.

No paragraph of this publication may be reproduced, copied or transmitted save with written permission or in accordance with the provisions of the Copyright, Designs and Patents Act 1988, or under the terms of any licence permitting limited copying issued by the Copyright Licensing Agency, 90 Tottenham Court Road, London W1T 4LP.

Any person who does any unauthorized act in relation to this publication may be liable to criminal prosecution and civil claims for damages.

The authors have asserted their rights to be identified as the authors of this work in accordance with the Copyright, Designs and Patents Act 1988.

First published 2004 by
PALGRAVE MACMILLAN
Houndmills, Basingstoke, Hampshire RG21 6XS and
175 Fifth Avenue, New York, N.Y. 10010
Companies and representatives throughout the world

PALGRAVE MACMILLAN is the global academic imprint of the Palgrave Macmillan division of St. Martin's Press, LLC and of Palgrave Macmillan Ltd. Macmillan® is a registered trademark in the United States, United Kingdom and other countries. Palgrave is a registered trademark in the European Union and other countries.

ISBN 1–4039–1722–1

This book is printed on paper suitable for recycling and made from fully managed and sustained forest sources.

A catalogue record for this book is available from the British Library.

Library of Congress Cataloging-in-Publication Data
Rae, Ian.
Singular and different: business in China past, present and future/Ian Rae, Morgen Witzel.
p. cm.
Includes bibliographical references and index.
ISBN 1–4039–1722–1 (cloth)
1. China – Commerce. 2. Business enterprises – China. 3. Corporate culture – China. 4. Organizational behaviour – China. 5. Intercultural communication – China. 6. Investments, Foreign – China. 7. China – History. 8. Language and culture – China. I. Witzel, Morgen. II. Title.
HF3836.5.R34 2004
330.951—dc22 2003065675

10 9 8 7 6 5 4 3 2 1
13 12 11 10 09 08 07 06 05 04

Printed and bound in Great Britain by
Antony Rowe Ltd, Chippenham and Eastbourne

UNIVERSITY OF BATH
LIBRARY
10 - 8 APR 2004
658(51)

Contents

Preface

No individual can ever fully understand China. By pooling our resources and ideas, we hope we have got a little closer. We have approached this subject from different perspectives. Ian Rae is a businessman who ran his own business in China and speaks and reads the language fluently. He is responsible for the chapters on culture, language, negotiating styles and history. Morgen Witzel is a business writer who also knows the region; he has written about economics, financial markets and joint ventures with foreign businesses. We have also added a chapter on how to find out more, and hope the book will not only inform but also entertain those who read it. Finally, we would like to thank our many friends, Chinese and Western, who have provided ideas and helped us shape our thinking over the years.

Ian Rae
Morgen Witzel

The People's Republic of China

1
Introduction

> The most full minute description could scarcely suffice to give you anything like an accurate idea of a market singular and different in many ways from all other.
>
> (John Matheson, Canton trader, 7 February 1821)

To say that China is a country in the midst of great change is to risk making a statement that is blindingly obvious. The upheaval that began 25 years ago, when the communist government of Deng Xiaoping first embarked upon the process of reform, has led to massive changes in the country. The landscape of its cities, many of which have been largely rebuilt, has changed forever. Society has changed too, with more personal freedom and personal opportunity. Even the political map of the country is changing, with the ruling Communist Party embracing capitalism and calling on business leaders to join the party and help build a new China using the tools of the market economy.

Nowhere has this change been more profound than in the world of commerce. Twenty-five years ago, the state dominated the economy of China. Foreigners wishing to do business there were tightly controlled. In most instances they could only conduct negotiations through a single state intermediary body that dealt in their particular line of business. Their travel and movement were heavily supervised, and steps were taken to limit contact with the local Chinese population. Negotiations were sometimes tortuous and almost always bureaucratic, and could last for days, weeks or longer. Transportation and accommodation varied greatly, sometimes they were even worse than in parts of the Third World.

A quarter of a century has seen much improvement. Transportation, especially by air, is now greatly improved; the ancient creaking Russian Ilyushins that used to ferry passengers from Beijing and Guangzhou to other parts of the country have mostly been replaced by modern Boeings. Rail travel is improving too, and there are now millions of cars on the roads of China (though this is a mixed blessing, as the roads themselves still leave much to be desired). Accommodation is ample and often of high quality. Any Western businessman or businesswoman who wishes to do business in China need only get on a plane and go there.

Once there, restrictions on internal travel and accommodation have all but vanished. Now one can go anywhere and talk to anyone. Instead of one or a handful of potential business partners, controlled or hand-picked by the state, there are tens, hundreds, thousands of possible partners and clients. Magazines devoted to business in China are full of advertisements by Chinese companies offering seemingly endless opportunities for business and profit for any Western firm prepared to invest in the country. Does all this mean that business in China has been made much easier? No; quite the contrary. The past 25 years have made business in China much harder.

At this point the reasonable reader will ask why this should be. The great opening-up of China, the liberalization of its economy, the exposure to Western business methods, the exposure of Chinese consumers to Western products and Western media, all these will surely have led China to become more like us? Theorists on globalization like to talk about 'convergence', the process whereby, driven by global market and media along with rising personal prosperity, everywhere is slowly becoming just like everywhere else.

Admittedly, there are signs of this in China. Western brand names still fill advertising space on television and billboards – though not as much space, perhaps, as five or six years ago. More people speak English: there are supposed to be more English speakers in China than there are in Britain, though the quality of their English ranges from bad to adequate, with only a few who speak the language really well. Western fashions in clothing, music, films and other ephemera have a highly visible profile in the big cities, though if you look closely you will find that Chinese music and film still have a robust following and are major industries in their own right. But some Western influence has rubbed off – that is to be expected.

Our argument is that, deep down, beneath the superficial things we read about and see on the street, China remains 'singular and different'. The Western influences we see are adaptations, things China has taken on board to suit its own needs. Nowhere is this more visible than in the world of business, where the Chinese have proved adept at learning Western methods of finance and accounting, marketing and so forth and then grafting these on to businesses that remain essentially Chinese in style and outlook. And why should this surprise us? A country with 3,000 years (at least) of continuous and uninterrupted cultural development does not throw away that culture in a quarter of a century. The patterns of behaviour and psychology and education and cultural conditioning that first emerged 500 years before the birth of Christ and have been reinforced and strengthened generation by generation ever since cannot be broken overnight. China remains China; it is not like the West, and there are few genuine signs that it will ever become like the West. China is evolving and changing very rapidly, but the direction it takes in the future will remain distinctively and identifiably Chinese.

This has huge consequences for all of us, but none more so than for the businessman or businesswoman getting on a plane at Heathrow or JFK with an attache case and a laptop computer, off to do business in China for the first time. The first fact that this person has to recognize is that China is different. Not wholly different, not all the time; but different enough that one cannot simply go to China and play the game by the same rules as at home. Obvious things like language and culture stare us in the face on arrival, and we know we will have to work around these. But deeper down, there is a different psychology, a different approach to the problems and challenges of running a business. These differences spring from various sources: the history of the country and its culture; methods of education and training; the often very subtle role played by government; and so on. The nature and sources of some of these differences will be discussed in this book. But, to repeat, the first important step is to recognize that they are there.

These differences will cost you money. If there is a golden rule in business in China, it is this: everything you do takes twice as long, and costs twice as much, as originally planned. There is a corollary to the rule: your Chinese competitors may not be able to get things done any more quickly, but they can almost certainly do it cheaper. When Western firms first started going into China after the reform process, they had a lot of competitive advantages. First of all, they had better products, and could back these up with the romance and allure of Western brands and advertising. They had economies of scale. They had immense technological and managerial know-how, which enabled them to do business cheaply and efficiently.

Today, almost all of those advantages have gone. The superior products have been reverse engineered and re-designed, and now products nearly as good – occasionally better – are tumbling out of Chinese factories. The gap has been all but closed in advertising and branding.

The Chinese are learning new technologies very fast, and in some areas such as mobile telephony they are probably capable of producing products that are superior to Western brands. And, thanks to training programmes at home and overseas, not to mention the immensely valuable experience of working side-by-side with Western managers in joint ventures, the Chinese are also closing the gap in management expertise. There is still a shortage of trained managers able to work in big companies and against foreign competition, but compared to 25 years ago, progress has been immense.

Going into business in China always was a tough proposition, and it still is. The image persists in some quarters of hundreds of millions of Chinese eager to get their hands on Western consumer goods and grateful to pay any price for these luxuries. This is not so. Chinese consumers are very canny indeed; they know how to assess price and quality, and they are quick to spot a bad bargain. The glory days of marketing to the Chinese are over, if they ever existed. The emphasis now is on relocating manufacturing industries from the West to China, taking advantage of the skilled workforce and low wages to get unit costs down and make goods more competitive when re-exported to the West. But as we discuss later in the book, that advantage too is withering away.

Under the old system, everything was closed and there was no competition, but at least it was possible to identify fairly quickly to whom you needed to speak. The negotiations might be tough and labyrinthine, but once it was established that there was a buyer and a seller, a conclusion would usually be reached in the end. Today there might be a thousand potential partners. How do you identify them? How do you know which ones are best, most suitable, most trustworthy? If you can answer these questions, great, and hurrah for the free market. If you can't, then time and costs start to mount up and the golden opportunities start to recede towards the horizon. Bear in mind that you have to answer those questions in an environment that is linguistically, culturally and psychologically different from your own. Not completely different, not always, but just different enough to knock you off your bearings and create uncertainty. That is the time when even smart managers start making mistakes. The only way to deal with this problem is through knowledge, as much knowledge as you can possibly cram into yourself, about every aspect of China, no matter how tangential it might seem at the time.

We do not mean to sound pessimistic; our purpose rather is to be realistic. There are, of course, business opportunities in China, but it is important to be realistic about them. China's size and resources, both human and natural, are already having a huge impact on the world economy, and that impact is going to become even more pronounced as time passes. We cannot ignore China, even if we wanted to. The other alternative, then, is to learn as much about China as we can – remaining aware but ignorant is not really an option.

The purpose of this book is to discuss some of the ways that China is 'singular and different' and the consequences this has. The chapters that follow each touch on some aspect of that difference, be it background issues such as language, history and culture, or specifically business issues like negotiations, economics and financial markets. We consider the background issues to be just as important as the more purely business issues; the two sets of issues are intrinsically linked, and are equally important to understanding China. History, for example, has an entirely different relation to the Chinese psyche than it does to that of the West. Language has dimensions and connotations that are unknown to speakers and writers of Western languages. And these things in turn lead to different patterns of speech, thought and ideas that mean that when a Western person and a Chinese person sit down on opposite sides of a table, they often approach the subject of their discussions from a very different perspective.

We have chosen to emphasize particularly the history of China, especially its recent history. This is not something that is usual in books for businesspeople, who normally are not interested in anything historical. And generally in the West, you can get by doing business in other countries without knowing much about local history and politics (there are exceptions). But in China, history takes on a whole different dimension. A British historian, W.F. Jenner, writing not long after the reform process began in China, commented that the story of China thus far is dominated by two things: the history of tyranny, and the tyranny of history. Because of their long and continuous history – there have been no great breaks like the Fall of Rome or the Protestant Reformation, not for millennia – Chinese history seems somehow of a larger dimension. Certainly it exercises a far greater influence over Chinese thinking than Western history does over us.

The past one hundred years, have seen history bear down on China with a vengeance. The fall of the ancient Empire, the disasters of the Republic and the warlord era, the horrors of Japanese invasion and occupation, civil war, the Great Leap Forward, the Cultural Revolution: when so many millions died during the lifetimes of ourselves and our parents and grandparents. If the Chinese appear to treat reform with caution, if they are at times conservative in their approach, if they are not wholly receptive to things Western, we should consider that history and reflect accordingly. History is the key to understanding China.

There are, quite deliberately, no conclusions as such to this book, no single grand idea that will enable the reader to rush out, board a plane to China, and begin making money on arrival. Life is never that simple, and certainly not life in China. What we have endeavoured to provide instead is knowledge on a series of subjects that will, at some point if not necessarily immediately, be important in your Chinese experience. We have also put in a chapter on how to get information about China at the end of the book. Before one can start learning in detail about doing business in China, it is necessary to have some background against which to interpret more detailed information. We hope to provide at least some of that information here.

2

Why Is China So Important? And Why Is It So Important To Know About China?

In December 2001, after years of tortuous negotiations, the People's Republic of China was finally welcomed into the World Trade Organization as a full member. It was a surprisingly low-key event; the world was still preoccupied with the aftermath of September's terrorist attacks and the fighting in Afghanistan, and the signing of a trade agreement didn't even make the inside pages of many newspapers. Nevertheless, this was an event of immense importance. Of course, many of the details of exactly how China's economy will interact with the economies of other countries, especially those of the West, remain to be worked out. The devil is in the detail, as the saying goes, and it will be a long time before the real impact filters through.

Symbolically, though, China had arrived. Twenty-three years of economic reform brought China fully into the family of nations. Henceforth, China will increasingly expect – and perhaps demand – to be treated as an equal partner of the big economic powers, the USA, Japan and the European Union. And those powers will have to listen. China is no longer just a developing country. If present rates of growth continue, then in 10 years' time (maybe even less, depending on whose statistics you believe), the economy of China will be as big as that of Japan. Twenty years hence, it could be challenging the USA.

To be sure, that challenge could also be delayed. China is a big country with big problems. The pressing need to reform state-run industries, rising unemployment with its attendant evils, often poor, occasionally appalling industrial working conditions, an infrastructure that is often barely adequate, have been compounded by lack of popular representation in policy making, corruption within business and government circles and more recent and dramatic problems such as the SARS outbreak. Not everything is rosy in the Chinese garden, not by any means. But these problems are no greater than in many developing countries – and what sets China apart is that the government appears to be willing to face up to them.

Real attempts are being made to deal with the structural problems of the economy; they may or may not work, but no one can fairly accuse the government of not trying. There have been repeated attempts to crack down on corruption; again, only partially successful, but compare the problem of corruption in China with that in Russia, or indeed, Chinese anti-corruption drives with the draconian methods being employed in Russia by President Putin. And yes, there is no democracy to speak of in China, but there is no denying that the country is much more open than it was twenty years ago. Reactions to the SARS outbreak may have at first been inadequate and slow, but once the ball was rolling, information was made available to the public and dilatory officials were dismissed from their posts, including some at very high levels.

China has a big role to play in the world economy thanks to its size and population. It has vast natural resources, many of them as yet barely tapped. Its population are highly industrious and, at least in the urban areas, well-educated. In the past, rather simplistically, Westerners have tended to view China in terms of opportunities for themselves. The big population it was reasoned, must mean a big market for imported Western goods. A combination of natural resources and an educated population who would work for relatively low wages must mean a good place to locate production, and so on. This view assigned China a relatively passive role; it was a good country to go into, to sell things or make things. The symbolic importance of China's joining the WTO is that China is no longer just passive. It is an active player in the global economy – active, and beginning to flex its muscles.

Where China is concerned, globalization is not a one-way street. There are a lot of big Chinese companies, and many of them are getting even bigger. Already they are signing partnerships and setting up joint ventures with Western companies that will allow them to move into world markets. The era of the Chinese-based global company is on its way. In 2000, the list of the world's largest companies was dominated by US, Japanese and European firms. But by 2010 we will see at least a few Chinese companies making into the top 50; and by 2020, it would be no surprise to see at least one in the top ten.

Should we be worried about this? Only if we are not prepared for it. The big worry has to be that Western political leaders and Western business leaders will not recognize China's power until late in the day, and will then persist in the centuries-old Western tradition of seeing China in 'us and them' terms. This could lead to trade disputes, a return to protectionism, even diplomatic conflicts and sabre-rattling, which would be bad, not just for business, but for all of us.

We need China. Looking around at the moment, the other big economies are not looking so hot. Japan is flat-lining. Germany is sunk in gloom, still trying to figure out how to pay for reunification and how to deal with rising unemployment. US business is confused and lacking confidence, its managers distracted by post-Enron red tape and wrapped up in post-Enron guilt; recent polls show that many US managers no longer believe in what they are doing, or that their companies are acting in the best interests of society. Look around the world, and the economy of which country is still growing steadily, still performing well despite its occasional hiccups? That's right – China. If China doesn't do well, then East Asia falls apart, and if East Asia collapses (again), it will be the cue this time for a real global recession.

The role that China is playing, and will continue to play, is huge and complex. And, because China is 'singular and different', we can't simply treat it like any Western power, like one of the club, and build relationships and do business there just as we would anywhere else. Even the simplest beliefs about China often turn out to be wrong, simply because some of the usual rules don't apply there. (The fact that some others of the usual rules do apply, of course, just increases the confusion.) To get a better idea of the nature of China's role and importance – past, present and future – let's look briefly at some of the main issues: the size of the market, the pool of resources, and the prospect of 'Chinese globalization'.

One billion customers?

The opening up of China as part of the reforms begun in 1978 (these are discussed in more detail later in the book) was greeted with joy in the boardrooms of the West. China's huge population was seen as a natural market for Western imported goods, goods that the Chinese people had barely seen during the long years of near-isolation. Even staple household goods could be sold in China as, it was felt, the Chinese had been starved of novelty and any imported products would have a cachet. Those with long memories or a good sense of history remembered the good old days of the 1920s during the shambolic Chinese republic, when Western merchants had a field day in China and Western brands dominated the marketplace, at least in the big cities of eastern China. Now, from running shoes to automobiles, whisky to powdered fruit juice, ice cream to cosmetics, the global brand marketers of the 1980s were sure they could sell it.

For a while, some of them did very well. The 1980s were the days of the 'Wild East', when the rapidly growing Chinese middle classes bought Western goods purely for their novelty. Sometimes, they didn't even know what they were buying. Stories abounded of goods being used for purposes rather different than they were intended, like the Beijing bath-house offering its customers the opportunity to bathe in Nescafé. It seemed for a time that the Chinese appetite for Western goods was inexhaustible.

Problems started to appear almost at once, though. The first and biggest one, that hit everyone in the face immediately, was distribution. How do you ship goods around in a country the size of China, a single province of which can be larger than many European countries; particularly when transportation networks are unreliable or non-existent? It was easy to sell products; it was quite another thing to deliver them to customers. Western companies quickly learned to concentrate on a single centre, like Shanghai or Guangzhou (Canton), and the billion potential customers quickly dwindled to ten million or so.

This was, in retrospect, probably the right thing to do. Western firms began to enter the China market more cautiously, 'trying out' their approach in one of the big centres, making mistakes, learning from them, correcting the approach and then rolling out into other centres, building up their marketing and distribution systems slowly. Even today, though, only a few Western firms can accurately claim to have nation-wide distribution in China. Coca-Cola and Fosters do, but they use networks of Chinese distributors and have little or nothing to do with shipping their own products.

There were other problems. One, which emerged within a remarkably short time, was price resistance. The Chinese consumer in the street loved the novelty of Western goods, but was less happy about paying premiums of two, three or four times local prices to buy them. Here again there were exceptions. Luxury goods like high-range cars, cognac and fine wines could be sold at something like the same price they would command in the West. But for most firms, the delight in finding a vast untapped market was tempered by the realization that margins were going to be under pressure like never before.

The pressure on price was quickly increased by local competition. Thanks in part to joint ventures with Western manufacturers, Chinese businesses learned rapidly how to produce goods of very nearly as good – occasionally even better – quality than imported products. And they could do it far cheaper. So Western firms, seeing their goods priced out of the market, started setting up production facilities in China, to take advantage of the same low-cost base and get their prices down. They banked on their superior marketing know-how and sophisticated advertising techniques to keep their own brand profiles high. But the Chinese know at least as much, if not more, about mass communication than we do in the West. The Chinese government got involved too, providing money and support for top domestic producers in fields as diverse as bicycles, cigarettes, computers and alcoholic beverages. Domestic production rose rapidly. In white goods (fridges, washing machines and the like), domestic production now exceeds demand and price deflation has become a problem. The Western white goods makers who went into China in the middle of the 1990s had been blown out of the market by the end of the decade.

Most telling of all, Chinese consumers developed a very rapid resistance to junk. Dumping became quickly seen for what it was. There was a very brief holiday for consumer electronics makers, for example, when second-rate or out-of-date televisions and radios could be dumped on the Chinese market, but that did not last long. Chinese consumers are demanding, knowledgeable and price-conscious, and they tend by and large to know when they are being fobbed off with foreign rubbish. Quality is an issue of equal importance for Chinese consumers as for those in the West. The idea that Western goods could be sold on the back of novelty and brand name alone quickly dissipated.

Counterfeiting ate into the available market still further. It has been estimated that fewer than half of the branded running shoes sold in China are actually legitimate products. Software, music and computer games are also heavily pirated, despite sporadic government crackdowns. The Chinese government claims that some of the biggest buyers of counterfeited Western brands are Western tourists and businessmen, and given the numbers of European men in suits one sees going through the racks of CDs and DVDs in Chinese street markets, there may be some substance to this. But the problem is still there.

Far from striking the mother lode, then, Western marketers found they were scrambling for small market segments, and finding the competition extremely tough. Given other background problems, like the problem of repatriating earnings – which continued to be a headache into the mid-1990s – many scaled back their operations in China. Others dropped out altogether. A kind of managerial folklore arose about China, as the unsuccessful began to blame their failure on grasping government officials and unreliable business partners. 'You can't make money in China' was a refrain that began to be increasingly heard.

But you can make money in China, particularly if you are big and have plenty of resources, and time. Plenty of people have done so. Here are a few examples from the world of big business:

- Volkswagen set up its first joint venture with a Chinese auto maker in Shanghai in 1988. During the following decade, Shanghai Volkswagen built up a domestic marketing and distribution network in all the major centres of China. Volkswagens were marketed as reliable, high-quality and relatively cheap alternatives to direct imports, but better made than cars coming out of the old state-run auto plants. Taxi drivers, a big market in China, came increasingly to favour them. By 1998 it was estimated that Shanghai Volkswagen had 30 per cent of the Chinese car market – some estimates said even more – and the company was looked on with favour by local and national governments alike. While other car makers struggled to gain access, Volkswagen got privileged treatment. Volkswagen succeeded because it invested for the long term. It was many years before Shanghai Volkswagen made a profit (it is now very profitable indeed) but the company took the long view. And its managers invested in networks and relationships, not just in plant and production.
- IBM had a big presence in China before the 1949 revolution, and was one of the first Western companies back in after the 1979 reforms. It began by selling computer equipment and terminals to the Chinese government, and before long was being invited to bid on big infrastructure projects as China sought to modernize its antiquated telecommunications network. IBM's bids were often accepted, and business grew and grew, with more spin-off companies being set up. IBM also set up joint ventures with domestic companies in the burgeoning Chinese personal computer industry. IBM is one of the great Western success stories, but it has thrived by doing business in the Chinese way. Despite 20 years of experience in China and a trained cadre of Chinese managers, IBM China still prefers to do business by setting up joint ventures with local firms rather than simply establishing foreign subsidiary companies. IBM China thinks Chinese. And it makes money by doing so.
- Diamonds, in the West, are marketed as a symbol of romance, and producers like De Beers advertise diamonds as the ideal gift from a man to his wife, partner or girlfriend on a special occasion, such as

a wedding or an anniversary. Asian notions of romance, though, are somewhat different from those of the West, and De Beers had had a hard time of it when first beginning to market diamonds in Japan and Southeast Asia. Going into China for the first time, the company was more cautious. Its managers sat and studied the Chinese psyche. What, they asked, is a key value to which many Chinese aspire, and to which diamonds can be linked? The answer they came up with was 'harmony', one of the great Chinese virtues of classical times and an idea which still, wittingly or unwittingly, governs many people's thinking. Rather than love, then, De Beers decided to market diamonds as a symbol of an enduring relationship. Television advertisements were designed showing couples exchanging rings on their wedding day, and then flashing forward to show many years of happy and prosperous marriage in the future. By appealing to a distinctly Chinese virtue, De Beers has done very well; its busy shop in the fashionable Wangfujing district of Beijing is testimony to this.

For all the companies like these, there are dozens of other smaller, less high-profile companies making an excellent living out of selling specialist products or services into China. Some of these are very specialized indeed; like the English football club that went out to China in the mid-1990s, not to scout for players, but to offer training in football management to the hundreds of newly established Chinese clubs. The result of this spectacular piece of creative thinking: a profitable business and some very fine relationships with the Chinese football industry.

The idea of a billion customers is a myth. It probably always was. Chinese consumers are geographically scattered and personally diverse in terms of incomes, needs and buying habits. Marketing in China is not easy, and never really was, unless you got lucky. Clever companies can make money selling to China, but the fundamental principles apply there as elsewhere. They have to provide real value to consumers, and they have to target and promote to their customers in a realistic way. As the examples above show, the companies that are prepared to be creative and 'think Chinese', at least in a limited way, are the ones most likely to succeed. Because once you get over the initial hurdles, identify your market and find out what it wants and learn how to speak to it, the returns can be huge.

The size of the Chinese market is and remains important because for any given product or service, the segment that wants to buy it is likely to be comparatively large, possibly larger than in any single Western country. But standard marketing problems like price, advertising, competition and distribution are likely to be bigger as well. If the potential rewards are greater, then so too are the potential risks. This is what scares off some Western companies. But turn the statement over and think about it the other way: if the potential risks are great, then so too are the potential rewards. Despite all the problems, and despite the fact that the past is littered with the wreckage of companies that tried and failed in the China market, the potential is still there.

Workshop of the world?

Walk into any department store, pick up an item – particularly mass-produced things like toys and clothing, but increasingly also household appliances like vacuum cleaners – and the chances are increasingly good that you will see 'Made in China' on the label. Go past a souvenir stall and pick up a novelty item or postcard that reads 'Welcome to America', or 'God Save the Queen', or 'Vive la France' or whatever is appropriate to the country you are in. Turn it over, and there is every likelihood that it will have been made or printed in China.

In 1998, an American spy plane was forced down by the Chinese air force and compelled to land on the island of Hainan after it had apparently breached Chinese airspace. Hawks in Washington urged the Clinton administration to retaliate by putting embargoes on imports of Chinese goods. There was panic among American retailers, and the big multiples led by Wal-Mart lobbied vigorously against trade sanctions. They had discovered that 50–60 per cent of the goods they sold – more in some cases – were made in China. Putting up prices to cope with the costs of an embargo would spell ruin for them.

Increasingly, it is not just Chinese companies making cheap goods for export. Slowly, at first, in the early 1990s, but in ever-increasing numbers as the decade wore on, big and not-so-big Western companies shut down their factories in Britain and the USA and continental Europe and opened up new production plants in China. Some Japanese firms, struggling to make a profit during an apparently endless recession, started doing the same thing.

At the time of writing, this is the big trend as far as China goes. The impact on the world economy is quite staggering. In 2002, China's trade surplus with the rest of the world reached $100 billion. Most of that surplus went to the USA, whose trade deficit with China in the same year was $83 billion. And those numbers are going to get even bigger. The problem is starting to become a real concern to Western governments and economists. There is worry about the continued 'hollowing-out' of the Western industrial base as even famous brand names shut down home production facilities, putting local people out of work, and build new factories in China. The balance of payments is starting to become of concern as well. Meanwhile some fairly fantastic predictions are doing the rounds; according to one recent report circulated on the Internet, by 2010, 50 per cent of the world's consumer goods will be made in China.

So, is China the new workshop of the world, and should most Western business leaders be considering following the current example and relocating production from Birmingham to Beijing, from Wisconsin to Wuhan? As a strategic option it has to be considered, but in doing so there are a number of factors that need to be taken into account. There are attractions to operating in China, but there are also strong risks.

Cost risks

As we said in the introduction, everything in China takes twice as long and costs twice as much as originally planned. This is partly because our cultures are so different, and we have quite different conceptions of things like time and personal relationships; and, unless the Western party have some fluent Mandarin speakers in their midst, the language issue is bound to complicate things. More than one company of our acquaintance has planned and budgeted for establishing a plant or other business facility in China, and come to the sober realization – usually too late – that the costs were a lot greater than anticipated.

Wages, for example, have a habit of coming in a lot higher than projected. This is particularly true of wages for skilled and experienced managers. Chinese managers are in a seller's market as far as their own labour goes; there is nothing like enough fully trained managers to go around, especially not managers with experience of working in an international environment and with international partners. Those that do exist are quite happy to 'job hop', accepting offers for higher paid and more senior positions in other companies and leaving almost at a moment's notice. Companies, sensitive to this problem, in fact fuel the trend by offering ever higher wages and bonuses in an effort to retain key staff. Somehow, though, it never seems to work. One British electronics firm, setting up a factory in north China, hired three top managers, all with degrees and one with a PhD from an American university, and paid them 50 per cent over the going rate for such posts in China. All in vain; within six months two of them were gone, and by the end of the year the third man, frustrated by the lack of qualified managers to work with, had handed in his notice as well. The plant, which lacked senior managers of any kind for several months, virtually ceased production until a British expatriate team could be flown in – at vast expense – to turn things around.

More generally, history tells us that this kind of competitive advantage never lasts for long. The combination of high skills and low wages is not sustainable. Foreign firms that rush in to take advantage of low wages create a dynamic labour market, in which wages and general prosperity rise. Soon, wages are on a par with other developed companies. It happened in Japan, HongKong and Taiwan, and was well on its way to happening in Korea, Malaysia and Thailand before the Asia Crisis of the late 1990s set things back, but will happen there before long too. And the cycles are faster now. How long until China's costs rise to equal those of Britain and America? Will everyone be moving back again in ten years?

Probably not, because within China's vast space there are substantial inequalities between the comparatively well-to-do east and the poorer west, and as wages rise in the east more companies will relocate towards the west. (But this relocation too will have its costs.) The current rush will slow and there will be more equilibrium. China's popularity as a workshop of the world is likely to last for a generation or so, all other things being equal. But the cost advantages to be gained from operating in China will wane slowly throughout that time.

Whatever one calculates the costs to be, the true costs of operating in China will always be higher than foreseen. Ample contingency funds will be required, and expectations of profit should be scaled back. That does not mean there is not profit to be made; it means, rather, that one should be realistic.

Competition risks

Of course, the benefits of operating in China are available to one's competitors as well as oneself. If the Acme Shoe Company moves to China and sets up a plant there and starts undercutting the Omega Shoe Company, the obvious response of the latter will be to move to China and start making shoes there as well. The price advantage over the competition then disappears. And meanwhile, the Yangtze Shoe Company is producing and exporting shoes at a cheaper price than both. The result is that prices of shoes world-wide begin to level out or even deflate. Great news for consumers, not so good for shareholders. Relocating production to China, or any other low-cost economy, gives price advantages only until the rest of the competition catches up and starts doing the same thing. Then one has to find some other way of differentiating from the rest of the market. The benefits of relocation are great while they last, but don't expect them to be permanent.

Environment and political risks

Much depends, of course, on whether China can be expected to remain politically stable. Since the bloodshed at Tiananmen in 1989, there have been no large-scale anti-government protests and recurrence remains most unlikely (recent events in HongKong have been largely of local concern). There are problems with Islamic extremists in the west of the country, but most of China's law and order problems are the product of purely criminal rather than political activity. Chinese cities remain among the safest in the world, general security is good, and internal political unrest is less than in most big European countries – there are no Chinese equivalents to the Real IRA, the Basque or Corsican Separatists, or the Red Brigades. In the early 1990s, especially after Tiananmen, Western futurologists spent a lot of time trying to predict what would happen to China. Among the possibilities considered were the gradual fragmenting of the country as areas slipped outside the control of central government, leading to a situation like the era of the warlords in the 1920s. Another possibility was that the government, with the aid of the People's Liberation Army, would crack down, bringing the era of reform to a close; reforms might not actually be repealed but no new liberalization would be allowed and the centralized communist state would remain in place.

As so often happens when futurologists get going, they ignored the third and least dramatic option, that the process of reform and liberalization would proceed slowly and in a measured manner, that central government would gradually and quietly open up, and that some powers would be devolved to the provinces while maintaining central authority. This is pretty much what has happened. The handing over of tax-raising powers to the provinces, for example, has been a big step in reducing central authority over everyday government, leaving the authority free to concentrate on policy. There has also been a slimming down of central government (it is now merely huge, not gargantuan as before), symbolized by the abolition of 13 government ministries in 1998. We talk a lot about leaner government in the West, but the Chinese appear to be trying to do something about it.

The government is also getting more confident in its ability to deal with dissidents and minority groups. In the early 1990s, dissidents were watched closely and arrested immediately if they spoke out of turn.

Now they are granted more leeway. Internet traffic in and out of anti-government websites is routinely monitored, but those logging-on to such sites are no longer automatically paid a visit by the police; traffic is allowed to continue so long as it is judged to be harmless. This ability to tolerate dissent at least in a limited form has extended to China's ethnic minorities. Under Mao, it was insisted that all residents of China were Chinese, or should become so at the first opportunity. But China, it appears, is now learning how to celebrate its ethnic diversity. By 1998, the revamped Shanghai Museum was devoting an entire floor to other ethnic cultures, especially Tibet; this would have been unthinkable two decades earlier. And at the Communist Party Congress of 2002, delegates from the ethnic regions of the south and west appeared in their own ethnic ceremonial garb, making a pleasing contrast to the black suits and garish ties of the rest of the group.

This is, of course, not just a matter of the Chinese government deciding to become warm and friendly towards ethnic minorities. There is an economic motive as well. With price deflation, people are no longer spending enough money on consumer goods to keep the domestic economy strong. So the government has hit on tourism as the next big thing. Urban Chinese of the north and east are being positively encouraged to travel to the south and west to see the riches their country has to offer. New public holidays have been created and people are being urged to get out and explore. In 2002 a new spring holiday was announced and promoted with the message that city people should go out and explore the country. The authorities estimated four million people would travel from the cities to the country over the course of the new holiday. Instead, nation-wide the total was closer to forty million, possibly even more. The public transport system could not cope, and overcrowded trains ran as much as ten hours late. In 2003, better prepared, the government made sure there were more trains and the situation was much better, and government even apologized for the confusion of the previous year.

The overall situation remains good, though things could still go wrong. Islamic extremism could worsen; it is just possible that popular grumbling in HongKong about the government of the Special Administrative Region could spill over into the rest of the country; factionalism could re-emerge within the Communist Party. It does not do to assume that things will be forever rosy in China, but many of the assessments of the political future of the country seem to be extremely unjustified. The political situation needs to be watched, but there are other and more urgent risks when operating in China that need attention.

Chinese globalization?

The third and final factor in China's growth that commands our attention is the gradually growing numbers of Chinese companies that are moving out of China into the global economy. There have been plenty of straws in the wind already. Chinese companies have been seeking capital overseas by listing on the New York, London and other international stock exchanges since the 1990s. Chinese businesses, working closely with the Chinese government, are quietly setting up partnerships in developing countries, building everything from railways in Africa to community centres in the Caribbean. The groundwork is being laid for something big.

The impact that Chinese investment can have on a country was shown graphically in Canada in the 1990s. Following Tiananmen Square, and with the prospect of reunification with China looming, prosperous residents of HongKong began preparing boltholes for themselves overseas. Many made for the west coast of Canada, where there was already a large overseas Chinese population. They sank their money into houses and invested in businesses, and in a matter of months created an economic boom in the hitherto depressed region around Victoria and Vancouver. House prices skyrocketed, and business real estate prices rose as well. Then came the handover, which went smoothly, and the pessimists realized that nothing much was going to change in HongKong, at least not in the short term, and they pulled most of their money out and came home again. The economy of the west coast of Canada fell back into recession.

Now, though, there is a more sustained effort going on to push Chinese businesses out into the world. In two industries in particular, computers and cars, Chinese companies are slowly tying themselves into the global industries. Most interesting of these recent moves was the signing of series of joint ventures between Brilliance China, China's largest domestically owned car maker, and several American and European manufacturers, notably BMW. The purpose of most of these ventures, in which Brilliance is a minority partner, is to allow it to learn the very sophisticated techniques of design and manufacture which are necessary to succeed in the bitterly competitive global car market. There is no doubt as to Brilliance's long-term aim. At some point in the future, cars with the Brilliance badge will go on sale in the USA and Europe. And why not? Japan did it, Korea did it, even Malaysia has done it. It might take a decade, but then these are companies and people who can play the long game. If not Brilliance then some company like it will go global in the car market.

Computer makers like Great Wall are also getting into position to reach into global markets, although interestingly there has been little interest in large-scale software development; here, India is the big rival to the West, while the Indians make very little computer hardware. We could speculate on the possible cultural reasons behind this, but it is better perhaps to think about where this trend could go next. One obvious possibility is all those struggling consumer goods makers, trying to compete in a country which is already overstocked with fridges and washing machines. Exporting white goods is the next logical step, followed by further expansion into overseas markets. Service providers are still a long way behind, but the future must exist for them as well.

Unless something very dramatic happens in the near future, we need to face reality: the Chinese are coming. How well we deal with the competition they will bring will depend on how much we know about China and Chinese ways of doing business. This means that even if you never intend to go to China or do business there, you still need to learn. The time to start learning is now.

3
All Under Heaven: The Growth of Culture and Society

The past is often present in China. You can see it in ancient irrigation systems or the dams and dykes holding back great rivers, the terraced padi fields on hillsides and the cultivated loess plateaux. There are also man-made artefacts such as the Great Wall, though few ancient buildings remain as the Chinese almost always built in wood. Present-day China has largely been re-built, and with the odd exception you will see little typically Chinese architecture apart from peasant homes. The place where the past largely dwells is in the people's minds; the past is an integral part of Chinese culture, and so of Chinese society. This is by no means a backward-looking denial of the present, but rather an acknowledgement of a tradition, a literature, a history, adumbrated by a code of conduct regulated by philosophers that has lasted well over 2000 years. So a young Chinese, Western-dressed, speaking English, working with computer technology, will probably know about Cao Cao, a hero of the Three Kingdoms circa AD 200, who was always so quick off the mark that he would arrive anywhere before you could say 'knife'. To this young person, Cao Cao and his men are just as real as Mao and his men on the Long March of 1934–5, or the actors he may watch in a television soap opera. China's past is taught in all schools, not just as history but as part of being Chinese. It impinges directly on everything that has happened ever since. It is regularly invoked; the most modern of contexts often contains an allusion or a quotation, as fresh today as two millennia or more ago.

There are legends of the mythical figures who founded China: Sui Ren who made fire, Fu Xi who taught the people how to fish and how to write, Shen Nung who taught them how to till the soil. Then came Huang Di the Yellow Emperor, whose name came from the colour of the earth, who measured time and introduced calendars, the sexagenary cycle or 60-year cycle still in use in some remote rural areas. He also introduced the compass, copper money and improved agriculture. He is regarded as the first great ruler of China, and to this day Chinese refer to themselves as sons and daughters of the Yellow Emperor. By now the Chinese were settled in the Yellow River basin where they established a secure base, beating off aboriginal tribes from outside. How much the history of these times is either true or accurate is open to question inasmuch as the Chief Minister of the Yellow Emperor is depicted as having four eyes. Two celebrated and wise rulers, Yao and Shun, noted for their benign rule and perspicacity, then followed, preceding the Xia dynasty founded by Emperor Yu, whose traditional dates are 2205–1766 BC, which is almost as shadowy as its predecessors. However, there is a legend of a great flood at this time which tallies with that of Noah's ark and other similar accounts elsewhere in the world. By the end of the Xia dynasty there were perhaps ten million people in a primitive organized society that tilled the soil. Then came the Shang dynasty, which most Chinese scholars accept as the beginning of recorded history. Over time society developed and population grew. Again little is known; there is evidence of decorated bronze utensils and some primitive drawings with simple inscriptions.

We must now fast-forward nearly a thousand years, well into the Zhou dynasty, which followed the Shang. The written language of ideograms and pictograms known as characters had more or less reached its present form. Society was more complex with carefully graded hierarchies of authority and responsibility. There were towns with small urban communities; as before and since, the bulk of the population were peasants who worked on the land, and this is still just true today. The first written work to survive from this time is the *Book of History* which recorded events from earliest times and also contained homilies attributed to Duke Zhou (10th century BC), whose *Book of Rites* is remembered still by giving his name to the marriage ceremony *Zhou Gong zhi li*. The *Book of Rites* also expounded a concept that has been important in Chinese eyes ever since, the Mandate of Heaven whereby the Emperor rules his subjects; should he rule badly, then he forfeits that right and should go. The people have a moral basis for action and this has been the reason underlying Chinese getting rid of bad rulers ever since, down to more modern times, though in recent years China's rulers have shown no sign of abdicating their posts, or accepting that such a principle applied to them. As the millennium progressed there were more historical works; the *Spring and Autumn Annals* and the *Intrigues of the Warring States*, both narrative chronicles of events, wars and rulers. Another work depicted the rulers of the day as robber barons and not fit to rule, all having forfeited the Mandate of Heaven. There was a collection of poems, the *Book of Odes*, which were based on the peoples' mood and contained some social protest, mainly at harsh working conditions, and also the *Elegies of Qu*, a polemic by a banished official who committed suicide by jumping into a river. He is still commemorated by the annual Dragon Boat Festival where huge long boats, each with a hundred oarsmen, with drums and gongs fore and aft, race each other in front of thousands in HongKong, where most people know the story well.

It was at about this time, say 500–300 BC, that there arose a group of men, some of noble birth, some scholars, some soldiers, all educated and some in official positions, who propounded theories of government, society and human relationships and duties. They taught how people had both rights and responsibilities towards each other and to the state. Their teachings were formalized and taught widely by disciples, in time forming the basis of a moral and social code that guided Chinese thinking more or less unchallenged until the end of empire, right up to the first Republic of 1912. Despite subsequent civil war, foreign war, more civil war and the revolution that then followed, they remain an influence to this day. Although these sayings and readings were venerated, even at times worshipped, and their content became an obligatory part of formal education, they never took the formal and social place that Christianity did in the West, or Islam in the Middle East, although their influence was at least comparable, if not more. In recent years new schools of thought have also left their mark on what is now an increasingly materialistic and atheistic society. It is interesting to note that the two ideas that have really stirred modern China, apart from patriotism, are both alien: communism and nationalism. These early teachings were completely Chinese and included what traditionally became known as the Confucian Canon, which consists of the Five Classics: the *Book of Changes*, the *Book of Odes*, the *Book of History*, the *Book of Rites* and the *Spring and Autumn Annals*, together with the Four Books: the *Analects*, the *Mencius*, the *Great Learning* and the *Doctrine of the Mean*. Some were edited by Confucius, some record his sayings, some quote him at length and parts of some have little to do with him. They were first translated and edited for English readers in the nineteenth century by a noted scholar and missionary, who wrote at the time how a Chinese he met asked if he too had a surname (i.e. did we Westerners also include the family name when introduced)?

Confucius, or Kungzi, Master Kung, is surely the best-known Chinese ever to have existed. He was given the Latinized form of his name by the

Jesuit fathers who settled in China in the late sixteenth century. Born in the state of Lu in 551 BC, he was a nobleman who reached high rank in government service, and was then forced to retire as a result of some intrigue at the age of 50. He went into a self-imposed exile and for the next 13 years travelled from state to state, expounding his ideas of social and political reform. At the time he had little success, as some rulers found his ideas eccentric, even dangerous as they could threaten authority by their calls for dutiful and righteous conduct on the part of those in power, and he died an apparent failure. His best known legacy is the *Analects* of Confucius, a collection of his sayings compiled by his disciples, in which he expresses what he believed his prime function: to interpret China's original cultural heritage, calling himself a transmitter and not an originator. However, in transmitting, he introduced his own moral concepts by which men should regulate their lives. Thus, in regard to society he considered functions should correspond to the names given to them, saying that the ruler should be ruler, the minister should be minister, the father, father, the son, son. In individual behaviour, Confucius emphasized what has been since translated as benevolence and righteousness, that is, each person fulfilling his role in society and doing what he ought to do. If a man does the right thing but for the wrong reasons then he is acting for profit, and his motives are wrong; so '*yi*/righteousness' and '*li*/profit', were diametrically opposed. Benevolence is the concept of man's duties in society and could mean consideration to others, thus 'do not do to others what you do not wish for yourself'. From righteousness came the idea of doing something for nothing; one should not shirk responsibilities. A superior man, for example, should try and enter politics because it is right for him to do so, even if he knows his principles cannot prevail.

Confucius described himself as 'one who knows he cannot succeed, yet keeps on trying'. He also believed in fate, which he interpreted as the will of heaven, saying that if his principles prevailed it was fate, but if they failed it was also fate. As regards the customs of the day, Confucius condemned human sacrifice, which was still practised, approved of ceremony and upheld social propriety. He described his own development: 'At fifteen I set my heart on learning, at thirty I could stand, at forty I had no doubts, at fifty I knew the decree of Heaven, at sixty I was obedient, at seventy I could follow the desires of my mind without overstepping the boundaries of what is right.' This, and many other sayings are regularly quoted to this day, not just in moral or theoretical works, but in everyday life. Subsequently Confucian thought was to be reinterpreted, added to, even formalized at one stage into a quasi-religion, but always maintained its great influence. It became the state religion under the Han Dynasty (after 200 BC) and Confucius was sometimes regarded as divine. His teaching imbued the scholar gentry who came to rule China, and the Confucian ethic guided actions and policies. He made no mention of any relations with other countries for he knew of none. China was, as now, the Middle Kingdom; the universe '*tianxia*/all under heaven'.

According to tradition, Mencius studied under Confucius' grandson and travelled widely preaching his ideas. The *Mencius* (another Jesuit Latinized name) is one of the Great Four Books, compiled some two hundred years later, and represents the more idealistic side of Confucian thinking, saying that man is by nature good and that everyone possesses intrinsic benevolence, or compassion, for others. Thus he said that 'man has four beginnings just as he has four limits' and these beginnings lead to benevolence, proprietary, righteousness and wisdom. So one should 'treat the aged in your family as they should be treated and extend this treatment to the aged of other people's families...' In politics, he repeated the maxim that if a ruler did not act as he should, then indeed the people had the right to rebel. Good rulers ruled with moral instruction and education, bad rulers or military dictators through force. Mencius held up as an example of compassion the king who even went so far as not being able to bear seeing an ox led to sacrifice. Mencius also considered ability more important than heredity in choosing a ruler, though this was contained by his belief in stability and preserving the existing order; he also advocated a well-managed economy since hungry people could not be expected to be moral. When he spoke of heaven he said a man should follow the way of righteousness and in time he would achieve understanding. Perhaps much of Mencius' theory could be defined as believing that virtue brings success. Much of his work is presented as a dialogue. In the first passage he tells the king not to assume his presence at his court would necessarily be of use or profit. He later chides the King for using the word 'profit', saying he should concentrate on benevolence and righteousness. Nowadays a good proportion of educated Chinese know the opening remarks of this famous passage by heart, and on occasion quote it.

Two less well-known though important philosophers were Modi (Mozi) and Xunzi, neither of whose names were subsequently Latinized by the Jesuits, possibly because they were lesser known figures. Modi preached in opposition to Confucius in that he did not accept the established order. Tradition has it that he was a sort of wandering knight who in troubled times offered his services to anyone who could pay for them. He rejected Confucianism for its support of funerals, rites and ceremony, the trappings of tradition, also saying that the acceptance of fate would make people lose their will to improve their lot. His general premise was that benevolence and righteousness were an all-embracing love, so that everyone on earth should love everyone else equally, judging all values by the standard of being 'beneficial to the country and the people'. There seem to be overtones of a sort of early socialism; yet another of his sayings goes 'always agree with the superior, never follow the inferior'. Xunzi was the fourth great figure among the Zhou philosophers; his thought is the antithesis of Mencius and a rather trite generalization is that if Mencius was on the left wing of Confucianism, Xunzi was on the right. He believed human nature was originally evil, not so much a doctrine of original sin, but rather that everything that is good and valuable comes as a result of human effort, thus 'the nature of man is evil, his goodness is acquired training'. He further argued that any man could become great because he is originally intelligent and has the capability to do great things, and should live according to an agreed system and a social order, thus emphasizing the rules of conduct expounded by Confucius. Xunzi was an authoritarian who believed that men should better themselves through their own exertions. All these four great scholars were the same in wishing to preserve the existing order, to improve it if possible but not to overthrow it; a stable system for the benefit of all, where each one had his place and knew his responsibilities.

There was also another school of thought which was quite different in outlook and teaching. The Legalists, at a time of war between the various states, around 200 BC, taught a theory and method of organization and leadership on strictly totalitarian lines. The first exponent was Lord Shang, but he was followed and outstripped by Han Feizi, the outstanding exponent of the school, a nobleman of royal blood who had studied under Xunzi. It was as advisor to the famous and ferocious Qin emperor, often compared by Chinese to Mao Zedong, and the first to conquer all China of the time and impose a rigorous control system, that he made his mark (although he was murdered by a rival before the emperor ascended the throne). It is said that the Qin ruler, reading one of his essays, said that if only he could meet Han Feizi he would not have lived in vain. The Legalists did not, like other philosophers, appeal to the past to justify the present, considering new problems needed new measures. It was not enough to depend on men doing good by themselves, rather it was necessary to bring it about they can do no wrong: 'He who rules a country ... does not concern himself with virtue but with law.' This in turn implied a capable ruler but that too can be achieved by method, and in turn the right men can be found to do everything for him. So an individual was held directly responsible for carrying out, exactly, the duties implied in his office. If he performed them well he was rewarded, if badly, mercilessly punished. There is the tale of a courtier who moved the king's hat to shade his face as he slept in the sun. On waking, the king had him executed as he had usurped the duties of the Keeper of the Royal Hat. Since retribution was meted out to failures, then no one who was not confident would dare take any job offered in the first place. Thus the ruler could rule by 'doing nothing, yet there is nothing that is not done'. This ferocious doctrine played a major part in ensuring Qin supremacy over the other states; the Qin Emperor created a centralized administration, burnt all the literature of which he disapproved and terrified many of the population. He won wars against all his neighbours and finally built an enormous mausoleum where he lies buried with the famous terracotta army of his soldiers, and the bones of all the slaves who were buried with him, having died of apoplexy in his quest for the elixir of life. He was also admired by certain right-wing politicians in the 1930s who saw in his organized control systems and ruthless measures an early fascism.

The third great philosophy of the time was completely different in aim and method. The starting point of Taoist (Daoist) philosophy is the preservation of life and the avoidance of injury. Its first protagonist was an obscure recluse; it implied a negative form of escapism and a need to understand basic laws of the universe; and was not concerned with society, duties and responsibilities. Early Taoism was then expanded and promoted in the *Dao De Jing*, attributed to Laotse who lived about 500 BC, who said that Tao (Dao), the Way, lay hidden and was nameless and that 'the conquest of the world comes invariably from doing nothing' (there is another famous Taoist saying that goes 'Do nothing, and there is nothing that is not done'). The fundamental law of nature was that when a thing reaches one extreme, it reverts from it; from this it supposedly followed that 'diminish a thing and it will increase. Increase a thing and it will diminish', or again, 'All things stem from being, being stems from non-being.' From this it followed that if one did not acknowledge the existence of a problem, then that problem would go away, and also that 'he who speaks does not know, he who knows does not speak.' There were also the concepts of *yin* and *yang*, the two opposite forces to which everything belonged, the one meaning dark, inside, female, the other bright, strength, male. These provided a view of the cosmos which contained five elements, and this gave rise to the

Five Virtues and a mystic numerology based on five for calculating auspicious days. It also caused debate when Ming dynasty astronomers (circa AD 1500) found a sixth planet in the sky, as it did not fit in to what was by then seen as the established order of things.

From these general ideas there evolved a political theory in which the sage ruler rules well by doing little and troubles are caused, not because things are not done, but because too much is done. Thus 'the more laws are promulgated, the more thieves and banditry there will be', so 'banish wisdom, discard knowledge and the people will be benefited a hundred fold…' Not surprisingly, Taoism never became a state religion as such, though it has exerted considerable influence to this day. It has motivated various sects and movements, including the fanatical Boxers, an anti-foreign movement that attacked Westerners and Chinese Christian converts alike in North China in 1900, who worshipped Taoist gods and chanted Taoist incantations before going into battle. Another great Taoist philosopher, Zhuangzi, preached that man must have free and full exercise of his natural ability, thus laws, institutions and governments were attempts to establish uniformity and suppress difference, and people were better off without them. Another illogicality was that death need not be feared if the universe and the nature of things was understood. This Taoist school of thought held great appeal and later was formalized into a religion, interlarded with mystery and magic, which continues to this day. You can still see Taoist priests and temples in China. Taoism appeals to a surprisingly fey side to the Chinese psyche, perhaps because it offers a respite from the realities of living. There are also Taoist overtones to traditional Chinese physical exercises, swordplay and wrestling, now also to be seen regularly on film and television. Until about the second century BC there had been no formal organized religion with doctrine and ceremony. The primitive beliefs of the early Zhou, before Confucius, were based on worship of the spirits of the dead and the forces of nature, also divination, demonstrated by the so-called oracle bones with primitive carved pictographs of the still earlier Shang. Later Zhou people had the concept of '*tian*/heaven', the punishment of wrongdoing and the reward of virtue. All schools of thought had enjoined respect for ancestors which was later formalized into ancestor worship.

By the time of the Han Emperor Wu Di, 206 BC, an enduring pattern of society and government, which was to last until just over a hundred years ago, had began to emerge. Up till then all Chinese development had been entirely internal and divorced from any outside influence. At the bottom were the peasantry grouped in villages, some bonded, mostly free, who tilled the soil and looked to the local squire, a member of a class that came to be known as 'scholar gentry', for leadership and support. The scholar gentry were mostly literate and numerate, conscious of their responsibilities and duties to those above and below. They reported hierarchically to the provincial viceroy, who in turn memorialized the Emperor, the Son of Heaven. The scholar gentry were not only responsible for general administration and law and order, but the undertaking of public works. They were imbued with the Confucian ethic, all of which they studied and long parts of which they learned by rote. Advancement was largely through learning, and in theory, though very seldom in practice, anyone, even the humblest, could sit the imperial examinations. In practice it was just about impossible for a poor boy to gain admittance unless he had a patron. There were numerous tales of youths entering the examination hall and miraculously knowing all the answers. Some who sat the exams were over 70: there were no age limits either way. For about two thousand years this basic system ruled China, mostly well. It inculcated a respect for learning and an appreciation of the past, together with a cultural unity that remain to this day. The recent Cultural Revolution (1966–72) was not in this tradition. It was an aberration which sought to destroy the Party and social system of China by smashing the old in education, culture and custom. Culture was badly damaged but survived.

The written character *Han* that embraces China's first great dynasty also represents the Chinese race and the Chinese language and is nowadays in constant daily use. All Chinese are Hans who speak the Han language. Meanwhile, by about this time a very few adventurous Chinese had travelled West to barbarian lands in central Asia and one or two had got even further. Certainly there were, by this time, tales in Rome of a great land far to the East, reached by an overland route, later known as the Silk Road, running right across Asia. There were one or two unconfirmed rumours of travellers from the West reaching China, including a troupe of jugglers in Loyang who were said to have come from Rome. All roads to China were difficult; however, some intrepid Indians including a couple of Buddhists scaled the great mountains and reached the Han Court. The tale goes that the Emperor then had a dream which impelled him to send envoys to find out more about this new religion. Travelling to India via hostile barbarian lands, they eventually returned bringing with them Indian priests who were housed in a temple at court. Initially, the Chinese considered Buddhism as an occult belief not far from the mysticism of *yin–yang* or the magic of religious Taoism, and the theory arose that Buddha was in reality a disciple of Laotse; later on, many Buddhist writings were rendered into Chinese, and a steady stream of priests crossed the passes on the long journey from India. Buddhism came to be widely accepted, albeit mixed with native Chinese Taoism; later the Emperor himself was converted and Buddhism joined Confucianism and Taoism as one of the three great religions of China, and also became China's first great borrowing from outside. Its main concept is that the life of a being is only one aspect in the cycle of cause and effect; death then is not the end, just another aspect of the process. What a person is now is an aspect of his past life, what he does now will determine his future life. Buddhism offered a form of life after death, hitherto not considered in Chinese thought; it offered salvation to the good and implied retribution to the wicked, not everlasting, just a temporary purgatory. It was tolerant and flexible, accommodating up to a point Confucianism, filial piety and often local customs and beliefs.

The arts also developed, but never as much as the literature of China. The Chinese view of art was that it should not only represent the present but remind people of the virtues of their great ancestors, usually depicted in stylized form. Pictorial art and design is as old as the first relics of settlement and preceded any written records. A well-designed three-legged clay jug, estimated at being 4,000 to 5,000 years old, has been dug up in Shandong province; by the time of the Shang, say 3,500 years ago, there were bronze wine pourers and pots decorated with dragons and monsters. Later were jade carvings, lacquer paintings, ornamented pottery, bronze vessels and mirrors with intricate designs on the back with the written characters of the time, often rendered in a highly decorative form. The nature of the written language is that it lends itself readily to decoration; calligraphy can be an art form in itself. Imperial expansion under the Han then brought more contact with the edges of China. There is a strong influence of the Xiongnu barbarians, the powerful tribes on the borders, on bronze plaques found in the north west, and statuettes were made portraying the horses brought in from Ferghana, the central Asian market, in the first century AD. A realistic pictorial art, serving the upper classes, was in being by about AD 200, and the earliest landscape paintings to survive are scrolls dating from about AD 400. It was also at about this time that paintings with the Chinese brush became common, and there are scenes, mostly on brick, of people, huntsmen, archers and animals. The advent of Buddhism introduced a new theme; the Buddha, carved in many forms and often in a huge size all over China. Artists also began to paint scenery, not so much as decoration, but rather as subjects for contemplation. Pictures on silk scrolls were kept rolled up and only brought out to view on occasion, rather as the opening of a book. The painters of landscape did not go out in the open to sketch the subject, they worked entirely from memory, a tradition of admiring the past and working from it that continued so strongly and for so long that Chinese art became increasingly stylized. Neither art nor music ever equalled the literature of ancient China, and this remains generally true to this day.

For another 1,500 years or so China progressed and grew, led by a series of competent rulers and great dynasties, adhering to the same rules of conduct and concept of society, supreme in isolation. It was in fact the *Zhongguo* or 'Middle Kingdom', and it admitted of no equal. China developed a substantial pre-modern industry, remarkably advanced methods of agriculture and irrigation, medical treatment, scientific and technical expertise, a system of banking and postal services. Huge cities of up to two million people, larger than in Europe, were efficiently administered, a system of canals linked north and south, roads were well-maintained. Beyond the frontiers, the barbarian tribes were kept away or cautiously absorbed into Chinese culture and so Sinicized. It was when the barbarians learned Chinese ways and military techniques that they became truly dangerous. When their lands were occupied, as in South China, in time the inhabitants became part of the Empire. There were of course long periods when things did not go well such as later occupation by the Mongols of all North China in the thirteenth century, but this did not last. Genghis Khan established a huge empire from central Asia right across China; the only territory under Chinese rule was south of the Yangzi. The Mongols, as the saying went, 'saw the world on horseback', and they stayed in China some 80 years. Literature and debate flourished throughout this time, and poetry and prose did likewise. With the Tang, which later followed the Han, China reached her zenith culturally, socially, politically and this is still remembered as such to this day. The Cantonese still call themselves men of Tong (the Cantonese pronunciation of the character Tang) and any district inhabited by Chinese outside China, called 'Chinatown' by Westerners, is really the territory of the Tang. Then came the Song dynasty, when Chinese science and technology was at its peak, astronomers scanned the heavens, scholars debated the great philosophers, and China was at an intellectual highpoint.

Apart from the effect of an enormous increase in population, the basic concepts of society and culture remained fairly constant. Chinese remained innovative, new ideas were welcome, people wrote, and thought. Then, beginning about the year AD 1300 or so, there came an imperceptible change. Society slowly became more inward-looking, accepting the past as an immutable model and rejecting change and innovation. This was becoming evident by the time of the Ming, whose middle years corresponded with the Renaissance in Europe. The magnificent machinery of government still worked well, always provided there were competent people at the top; the country was fed, goods were transported, a vast army of a million men was trained and administered. The only new literature of note was a series of novels, read regularly today, of which the best known is *All Men are Brothers*, a sort of Chinese Robin Hood which is said to have been Mao's favourite reading in his guerrilla days. Junks ventured on voyages of exploration and rulers of bordering states, Korea, Annam (now part of Vietnam), Burma sent tribute to the court and made obeisance to the Emperor. But men no longer looked for something new to think about. There is a theory that all this came about because things were going so well so there was no need to look further, the so-called 'high equilibrium trap', though it is also said that necessity is the mother of invention. This inward-looking tendency turned to stagnation and in turn this affected society and administration. Other factors, such as intellectual conformism, also contributed to an insidious decay which had already set in when the first freebooting Western ships called. The rest was downhill, arrested only by violent change.

An integral part of old China was its social system, with its roots in antiquity. This system is now under the pressure of modern times, though some of its traditions and inborn attitudes exist to this day. The family system took shape during the Han dynasty, over 2,000 years ago, and endured largely untouched until the late nineteenth century; despite foreign wars and some Western influence, it remained fairly intact until 1949, even then surviving in part a new Communist society. Respect for parents, grandparents and all older relatives remains largely the rule; in no other country has old age been more honoured. There were two main reasons for this unique feature of Chinese civilization. The first was the great influence of Confucius, who considered the family to be the state in miniature, reinforced by the doctrine of filial piety and the worship of ancestors. The second cause was the comparative absence of any disruptive nationalism or regional loyalties, as developed in Europe and other parts of Asia. All China was ruled by the Son of Heaven, the Emperor, over a society made up of thousands of virtually self-governing communities, each in turn composed of family units. The local clan, sometimes consisting of a village in which everyone bore the same surname, kept an ancestral hall; in it were tablets to commemorate its forebears, to be visited and honoured at festivals and anniversaries. Each family in turn had a place set aside for this, and ancestral graves were sited in the nearby fields. Each clan had an income derived from commonly held land; this was used to provide help to widows, pensions for the aged, education for boys; thus providing an early welfare system whereby, in theory, no one would go destitute. In time of peace and order the system worked excellently.

However, since communications over such great distances were slow, and at times uncertain, efficient government depended almost entirely upon delegation of authority, plus the willingness of the people to accept that authority. Any major breakdown, natural disaster, famine, plague, or rebellion could cause a major disruption which even a strong and efficient central authority would take much time and effort to repair. If the central authority was weak or incompetent, there was disaster.

Family authority was vested in the father, but women, although without formal rights, had a great degree of influence, particularly in domestic matters. Sometimes they went much further. There were several famous Empresses, not allowed by convention to be seen by men, who stood behind a screen at court, but yet ruled through sheer force of personality together with scheming and intrigue. In nearly all families marriages were arranged, and the bride had a hard time if she did not get on with her mother-in-law. The first duty of any married couple was to produce an heir, if none was forthcoming one was adopted, or if the man was rich enough he would take a second wife or concubine. The village temple was the community centre, meeting place and administrative focus for local public works, tax collection and settlement of minor debts, and also a place of worship. Any problem of a more weighty nature, such as the punishment of a thief or a dispute over an inheritance, was referred to the magistrate. A similar system prevailed in the towns, but with more direct official control. The family system was one of the chief reasons for the basic stability of Chinese society through the centuries. It also developed the Chinese aptitude for collective living and conformity, much in evidence in recent years, such as for example the general acceptance of People's Communes established by Mao with the hope of boosting production, where men and women slept in dormitories and ate in huge mess halls. A grave weakness has always been that the strength of family ties and obligation led to corruption of officials; once a man was in a position to help his friends and relatives, the pressures on him to do so were very hard to resist. In Chinese eyes, loyalty to the family and the clan often transcended loyalty to the state.

Unlike other pre-modern societies, China never had the sharp cleavage between the bureaucracy, the landed nobility and the learned class which was often also the priesthood. The overwhelming majority of the scholar gentry were both literate and numerate, but some of the temple monks were not. In Europe most learning was in the monastery through the monks, in China it was in the *yamen* or courtyard of the gentry. It was the cultural unity and moral code of these educated administrators that held together this vast Chinese Empire. Thus the true aristocracy in China has been called the aristocracy of learning. Under them, in order, came farmers, craftsmen and merchants; professional soldiers were not even included, though wars were frequent. The old saying, now very much out of vogue, was that 'good iron did not make a nail, nor a good man a soldier'. The peasant was often free, not a serf, and possibly owned a tiny plot of land and his taxes, when fairly administered, were light. He was, of course, also dependent on nature; and in bad times the victim of oppressive officials and marauding brigands.

A clearly defined system and code of conduct, observed by all, made for long-term stability. A government largely based on duties and responsibilities ensured the people's welfare. Mostly it all worked well until a later decay set in, exacerbated by outside challenges, especially from the West. Finally the system collapsed, to be followed by over a hundred years of turmoil, which ended only recently.

4

The Language of the Han: Writing and Speaking Chinese

The nature and evolution of the Chinese language are fundamental to Chinese culture and society. The great philosophers who established a written code of conduct which for over 2,000 years guided the conduct of government and human relationships probably had a greater effect on shaping Chinese thought and attitude than has any other major language or any other culture, more than Latin and Greek on Europe, or Sanskrit on India. Nowhere else is the written word still held in such high esteem. Chinese is one of the most ancient, difficult, complex and yet efficient languages to exist. It largely ignores formal grammar and syntax, relying on word order and particles to indicate tense and order. It is written in a series of symbols or ideographs known as characters, each expressing a word and possessing an intrinsic monosyllabic pronunciation and tone, both of which vary widely according to which part of China the speaker is from. The simplest character consists of one stroke, the most complicated has 48. There are about 7,000 to 8,000 in general use and it needs about 3,000 to read a newspaper. Each has its own meaning and each one has to be learned individually. This written language is common to all Chinese wherever they may be; it does not necessarily relate to the sound of what is said, and there is little concordance between sound and symbol. It is therefore possible to learn to read and write Chinese without being able to speak a word. The spoken language varies widely but has a common syntax and structure. The variety and flexibility of Chinese means there is nothing new, technical, scientific, philosophical, political or social that cannot be expressed.

A tone is the pitch or level at which a word is pronounced, and is inherent. It is not the same as a sound which can be uttered in a different tone. Tones may rise, fall, do both, or be level; say one wrongly and it may represent something quite different and so another meaning. All characters have their intrinsic sound and tone in which they must be pronounced when spoken. The wrong tone may result in the wrong character. A character is a written symbol that represents a one syllable word, for that is the basic structure of the language; however modern Chinese is mostly in a series of two or three characters strung together, each of these characters retaining its own meaning, sound and tone. When linked with one or two other characters, the compound so created has a different, but related, meaning.

Character writing can be an art in itself with calligraphers executing various styles by brush, though modern China writes mostly with a ball-point pen. However, penmanship is still esteemed and a good hand may excite comment. The actual writing of a character consists of executing strokes to a certain order and design which in each case has to be learned. Many characters are themselves made up from other characters. Like-sounding characters may sometimes look alike, similar characters may have similar meanings. There are no certain rules or guidelines for composing characters; it is however sometimes possible to guess the meaning by context or components. Above all, there is no way you can spell Chinese, nor are there any shortcuts.

The very first written Chinese was essentially a picture language, with drawings depicting basic things such as fire, wood, sun, horse, cart, man, woman and so on. Clearly such written symbols were inadequate, and in time separate individual items were joined together to form a new character, to express an idea that could not be described pictorially. Thus there is a character for roof and a character for woman, place one over the other and you have one woman under one roof, which means peace. Other simple examples include: a man standing by the character for speech meaning a written missive, the sun and the moon together mean brightness, two trees mean a wood, three trees mean a forest, a bird and a mouth mean to sing, strength and field mean male and many more. But of course this too was inadequate as society advanced, and in time more and more characters had to be invented, often quite arbitrarily, or if there was a logic it is no longer discernible today. Characters, or parts of characters, were combined in various juxtapositions to create totally new ones; the radical or prime part denoting sometimes the general field of meaning, what is misleadingly called the phonetic, which only sometimes gives the sound. Characters in fact have to be learned as is, and there are no shortcuts. There are one or two systems to learning, but they are cumbersome. In general, aids to studying Chinese characters are often too complex to be worthwhile; the student is arguably better off without them. The best-known analyses the structure of the strokes and their relationship and is difficult to master. It takes less time to learn the characters by rote.

The uniformity of the written does not extend to the spoken. The major dialects, while having roughly common roots and word order, are mostly mutually unintelligible; indeed they can be as far apart as, say, French to Spanish. A northerner from Beijing, whose native speech is Putonghua, the common tongue known in the West as Mandarin, cannot understand Cantonese or other South Eastern seaboard dialects such as those of Xiamen or Fuzhou. He will understand a little Shanghainese and other Yangzi river basin dialects. His interlocutors from the provinces will however mostly understand him and be able to reply in Mandarin, albeit accented, as this is now the national language, the *lingua franca* for all Chinese wherever they may be and taught since the 1950s in schools throughout non-Mandarin-speaking areas. A peculiarity common to all these Chinese spoken dialects is the paucity of different sounds; there are only about 400 in Mandarin, for example. Over time the tonal system evolved, thus increasing the range of sounds; each major dialect now has from four to nine such tones. Mandarin, the common tongue, has four; thus 1,600 different sounds, still not many, as against about three times the number in English. The bizarre situation will arise whereby several written characters, all different in construction and meaning, will share an identical sound and tone and so if read out loud, separately and not in context, may lead to confusion and misunderstanding. In practice, spoken and modern written Chinese is largely made up of compounds whereby meaning is confirmed by linkage and context. This also means the speaker from another province whose tones are inaccurate, or the foreign student who cannot master them, can usually (but not always) be understood.

The majority of the Han population are native Mandarin speakers, albeit with varying regional accents. There are however no class accents in China; all speak the same. The purest, or most correct form, is Peking Mandarin, and the best would probably be spoken by a native of the city who is also a graduate of the university. It is a pleasant, lilting tongue and speakers roll their r's, so when they speak English they sound American. Most Northern Chinese Mandarin speakers have difficulty learning the Southern dialects, chiefly due to pronunciation and the greater number of tones. The next major dialect, actually a language in its own right, is Cantonese, centred on Guangdong province (Guangdong means Broad East and encompasses HongKong and Macao as well). It is also spoken in parts of the neighbouring province of

Guangxi (Broad West), and overseas Chinese settlements in South East Asia. It is the first language of about 80 million people and its purest form is spoken in the provincial capital of Canton, with very considerable variations throughout the region. North of Macao is the Toishan dialect, which in San Francisco's Chinatown is still spoken in its late eighteenth-century form, a legacy of the earliest settlements on the west coast of North America. Nearby are the Four Districts, again with a distinct dialect, then there are the Hoklo, the Tanka who are boat people, and also the people of Swatow to the north of the province.

As you travel away from the epicentre, west, south or north, so the local speech gets further away from its standard form. The fundamental structure of Cantonese is the same as for Mandarin, as indeed is the case with the other main Chinese languages. However, not only are Cantonese and Mandarin mutually unintelligible due to the very widely differing pronunciation, but there are nine (arguably twelve) tones in Cantonese, so if it is easy to get it wrong in Mandarin it is easier still to get it wrong in Cantonese. Cantonese learn to speak Mandarin readily and do so now in increasing numbers in HongKong, particularly since the handover to China in 1997; a south-to-north conversion course takes about three months. But Cantonese have a distinctive accent and get certain sounds wrong, leading to the old saying, 'don't fear heaven, don't fear earth, only fear a Cantonese speaking Mandarin'. Say this in North China and everyone laughs, say it at dinner in Canton and there falls a leaden silence.

We have of course no idea what ancient Chinese sounded like, though scholars judging from poetic metre believe it was closer to Cantonese and other southern dialects, with a large tonal range and a consequent sing-song effect. The very first characters to be deciphered were on Shang dynasty oracle bones, about 1600 BC, and already show some organization as a written language. By about 500–400 BC, when Confucius, Mencius and Laotse flourished, writing reached its present form, that is to say the actual characters mostly looked as they do today. However, the order of writing characters and the composition of passages, possibly due to their formal nature, had meanwhile already begun to evolve into a classical style of expression quite distinct from the vernacular and this remained the chief method of written communication right up to the early days of the first Republic after 1912. This so-called classical Chinese is a terse yet flexible placement of characters, whereby meaning is extrapolated from interpreting individual characters, many of which have secondary as well as primary meanings and most of which function equally well as noun, verb, adjective or adverb.

It has been likened to a crossword puzzle in linguistics, with some of the clues being acronyms. A Chinese who wished to be literate not only had to learn the actual characters, usually by rote, but also an arcane written style quite different from that of his speech. Inevitably, literacy was limited to the few, the scholarly gentry who ran the empire and whose work in overseeing massive public works and agricultural development necessitated both command of the written language and, of course, numeracy.

Learning was not, as in mediaeval Europe and before, largely confined to a priesthood; it was in theory open to all, as any man (with a few exceptions) could sit the imperial examinations. However, only a very small fraction of the population was literate, and it was not until the so-called Literary Revolution of the 1920s, part of the rising tide of nationalism, that the Chinese language began to be written more or less in its spoken form. To this day the classical style still regularly appears in the form of '*chengyu*' or the four-character proverbs that occur in the newspapers and speeches by the leadership; as for example the four characters 'eyebrows flying, colours dancing' describing the people's indignation at the humiliation of the King of Yue in 500 BC, still used in a modern context. This king slept on firewood and ate gall as he planned his revenge on the Kingdom of Wu. It was particularly quoted to illustrate China's humiliation at the hands of the West during the first republic. The remarkable continuity and cultural unity implied in this unusual language is also illustrated by the fact that a modern educated Chinese will recognize practically all of the individual characters in a famous passage from, say, the *Analects* of Confucius (4th century BC), or the *Records of the Grand Historian* (1st century BC), and will grasp the general sense. He or she will read, albeit with some difficulty, Tang dynasty poetry (8th century AD), and have practically no trouble with semi-classical historical romances written in the fifteenth century such as *All Men are Brothers, Journey to the West* or the later *Dream of the Red Chamber*, great stories known to all, and even now still occasionally told by village storytellers. Many English people have some difficulty with sixteenth-century Shakespeare and can only read fourteenth-century Chaucer in modernized form. (Anything earlier is a closed book; the English language only reached its present form at that time and a similar situation exists with other European languages.)

It usually takes longer to send or receive information in Chinese than in other languages. Such a complex language has in some ways proved a barrier to progress. For a start, no Chinese child knows enough characters to read a newspaper until he or she is at least 12. Even simple broadsheets for the peasantry, introduced by the Communists in the 1930s, called for at least 1,500 characters as against the 3,000-plus needed to read the average newspaper. Reformers have examined various options and it has even been debated whether to abolish the written characters altogether and replace them with the Roman alphabet. This was never seen as a serious option, as doing so would destroy the very essence of the language, apart from denying the entire past. And anyway, how does one spell a tone? It has in fact been done, in an outlandish Romanization that was briefly in vogue among academics 50 years ago; it was a remarkable system that indicated tonal change by inserting letters, thus a 'h' after the consonant was a level tone, a 'h' at the end a falling tone. Since then, an official Romanization has been introduced, known as *pinyin*, which spells the sounds and in which tones are indicated by diacritical marks. It is used, as well as characters, on maps, street signs and some public posters and is of help to foreigners, though most Chinese ignore it completely and are incapable of writing it. A more effective and far-reaching reform of the written language occurred in the 1950s and 1960s with the introduction of simplified versions of current characters, or in some cases, making one character do the work of two. In all, about 25 per cent of characters in common usage have been affected. If you learned the old version you can guess some, but not all, of the new as in certain cases the simplification was in informal use already. As with all such matters there was a political element to this; anything printed or published after a given date in the People's Republic would contain an element of simplified characters so its provenance was self-evident. The system came from Communist China and would be immediately proscribed in Taiwan, the losing side in the civil war, which to this day is different and clings entirely to the old. Other Chinese-speaking territories such as HongKong or Singapore, while also clinging to the old, accepted both systems.

The language also lends itself to modern communications. It is still possible to send a telegram in rural China; so how then do you transmit characters without an image or look up a word in a dictionary or a name in a phone book? How do you identify a character verbally, that is when talking on the phone? All are possible. In the late nineteenth century the China Telegraphic Code came into being and is still in diminishing use. The most frequently used characters are ranged in order, up to 9999, four digits for each. The message, in characters, is written in the corresponding numbers, and a series of four figure numbers are then transmitted; at the other end the receiving operator consults the code book and hands over a written message. Experienced operators know the common character code numbers by heart. To consult a dictionary or indeed a phone book, it is necessary to first identify the radical or prime part in the character that is sought. There are 214 of these, ranging from one stroke to many, and they are not always obviously identifiable although most Chinese know them automatically. The rest of the character will come to a given number of strokes, and the search then proceeds for characters with this number of further strokes under the appropriate numbered radical heading. As an example there is the character '*wu*', also a common surname and often sought in dictionary or phone book. You identify the radical component of this character which is '*kou*', the mouth radical, number 30. The next step is to count up the number of strokes remaining, four; you go through the characters under radical heading 30 with four more strokes and, lo and behold, you find '*wu*'. It so happens those four extra strokes themselves make up another character in its own right, '*tian*', heaven. So to make it clear on the phone which character you mean, you call it '*koutianwu*/mouth heaven *wu*'. Understandably, many people approach Chinese dictionaries and telephone books with reluctance.

Until quite recently, Chinese printers set individual type entirely by hand and a good compositor could set over 10,000 characters a day. It was said the more interesting the copy, the faster the setting. The various typefaces in use were, and are, known by number and name of a dynasty: thus New Song No 5, China's answer to 10 pt Times Roman. The computer and the word processor have now taken all this in their stride and a text in Chinese characters can be stored, though the nature and structure of the written language makes retrieval difficult, principally because there are so many different characters. Here the Romanized Chinese or *pinyin* is used for identification and read off into characters, which works well as long as the link between Romanized word and Chinese character is evident, usually by context. It can go wrong since the *pinyin* cannot differentiate between different characters that share the same sound. Right up until the beginning of the tweni-eth century, all Chinese was written or set vertically, columns right to left, so a book opened at the back. Then, with modern reform came writing left to right, which is usual practice today, though the vertical is still used in display heads and for space fitting. For some unexplained reason, occasionally notices and shop signs run right to left, and all you can do is have a go starting at each end. Another relatively recent change has been the adoption of Western punctuation and Arabic numerals. By far the easiest Chinese to read is the regular typeface of the printers font; personal handwriting can be difficult, and the so-called 'grass characters', a cursive running hand with strokes elided, are virtually impossible for the Westerner. It is still a token of esteem for a Chinese to give a scroll written by brush, in their own hand, to mark some event. It would be signed, dated, and contain a classical quotation.

There is no problem to writing Chinese in a modern context, where the old serves the new. By using long-established characters in relatively newly invented compounds, there is really nothing you cannot express in Chinese, including science and technology in all its forms. A simple example dating from the early twentieth century is '*zi lai shui bi*/self come water pen', i.e. fountain pen, more recently '*quan zhen*/transmit true', fax, or '*wei xing*/circling star', satellite. Philosophy, religion, politics, dogma of any sort are also covered; thus the conservative party is '*bao shou dang*/protect guard party', and the communist party is '*gong chan dang*/all together property party'. Or occasionally there can be a translation with a shift in nuance, thus '*min zhu*/people master', is democracy; a people's government, but not necessarily an elected one. Subtlety is shown with terms such as '*wei ji*/danger opportunity', for crisis. Some compounds are of course by no means new; a soldier in the People's Liberation Army is a '*zhanxi*/warrior', just as he was at the time of the Warring States over 2,000 years ago. There is also the matter of putting Western names into Chinese, or transliteration. The solution is to choose characters which when read out loud approximate to the sound, and have at best a good meaning or at worst a neutral one. So Churchill comes out as '*qiu ji er*' ('q' in *pinyin* equals 'ch') which is recognizable and means 'solid mound', but an outlandish '*yao gat yee*' which sounds nothing like it if these three characters are read in Cantonese. England is '*ing guo*/hero country', America '*mei guo*/beautiful country'; both sound about right and mean something pleasant. Advertising in all forms has called forth much ingenuity. The most famous ever slogan was coined long before World War II, rendering Coca Cola as '*ke kou ke le*/mouth thirsty getting joy'.

The difficulties that some of these alien structural concepts can cause the European student are exemplified in the experiences of the Jesuit priest, Matteo Ricci, who compiled a Chinese–Latin dictionary in Peking about the year 1600. On the left-hand page was a Latin verb with all its six persons and many tenses, some 30 or more entries; say the *amo, amas, amat* that schoolboys used to know. On the opposite, alone, one solitary character, '*ai*/love', covered the lot. So on it went, page after page. Yet the Jesuit fathers taught themselves written Chinese and some became accomplished scholars in their own right. At the time this was welcomed at the Imperial court, but later as relations with the West deteriorated so did contact diminish; by the early nineteenth century Chinese were largely forbidden to teach their language to foreigners, as part of official policy to keep the races apart. Few foreigners were at all interested anyway, and a later by-product of early European contact was the pidgin English of the nineteenth century which flourished until the 1930s in the coastal ports, becoming extinct as more Chinese began to learn English. With a basic vocabulary of a few hundred words, pidgin English was simple English according to Chinese spoken word order and usage. Thus, above was topside, below, bottomside and further was more far. To execute or carry out a task was to catch it, thus, 'me catchee breakfast, chop chop, right away'. Apart from a few missionaries no Westerners spoke any Chinese, and vice versa, so this was largely the means of communication between an expansionist West and a passive, though increasingly resistant, China. Official dealings were through a few, often inaccurate, interpreters and the opportunities for misunderstanding were immense. Sometimes of course this was deliberate. Lord Napier arrived in Peking in 1819 with banners transcribing his name into Chinese characters that read Laboriously Vile. The Hall in the Forbidden City, where the Emperor was obliged to receive the plenipotentiaries of the Western powers after the 1860 war and Chinese defeat was, unknown to them, entitled in large characters, Hall for the Reception of Foreign Tribute Bearers.

Today, apart from a very different attitude to the foreign language student, Westerners who learn Chinese have technology and expertise at hand that was denied their predecessors. Nonetheless, it is still not easy. The spoken language admittedly necessitates none of the tables and grammar called for in Europe; indeed a noun can qualify another noun, or denote action, what Sinologists call the verb-noun. Not only are there no declensions of nouns, tenses or moods of verb, but there are also no definite or indefinite articles, no agreement of adjective with noun, none of the paraphernalia of European language, or indeed of Japanese (which surprisingly has a totally different structure in spoken form). It is in fact difficult to parse a Chinese sentence along Western grammatical lines. But there are also different structural forms, such as there being no relative clause; you cannot say 'the man who came to dinner', it is 'came to dinner's man'. The tones present problems to some; being musical is not necessarily a help, being a mimic is. The real effort lies in the written language; characters have to be learned, by rote, writing each one out time and time again. As the student progresses he is heartened to find he is learning perhaps 30 or more a day; a week later he has forgotten most of them. Indeed, written Chinese is eminently forgettable for all, including Chinese. A Chinese who has been abroad a long while may hesitate over some characters as he writes home. The tried and tested learning method is to have character cards, with Chinese on one side, perhaps both regular and simplified version if applicable, with on the other the sound in Romanized Chinese and the meaning in English, with common compounds added. Your student is to be seen on train, bus or in a library alternately mumbling as he or she looks at one side of a card, then scribbling as he or she looks at the other.

The nature of the Chinese language lends itself well to symbolic expression. With different characters sharing the same sound, the range is considerable. As one example, the former leader, patriarch Deng Xiaoping's last two characters sound exactly the same as '*xiao*/little', '*ping*/bottle'. Thus a subtle hint of dissatisfaction with the leadership was the strewing of some broken bottles on Peking pavements. This punning of course extends to humour and many Chinese jokes are an untranslatable play on words. A current joke, which can bring tears to Chinese eyes, is the man at a dinner who refuses any wine as he has bronchitis, '*qi*/breath', '*guan*/tube', '*yan*/infection'. However, these three sounds can equally well mean '*qi*/wife', '*guan*/control', '*yan*/strict'. Chinese humour is seldom funny in English, but then ours does not usually translate either; Western attempts to tell jokes via interpreters are usually disastrous. One way round is for the approaching joke to be announced in advance; that way everyone laughs politely. It is interesting to note that whereas there are numerous Chinese terms denoting funny, laughable, amusing, there is no native term for humour as such. There are two characters reading '*ioumo*' an early example of the transliteration of foreign sounds. The word is often used in conversation, both as a noun as in English, but also a verb, but not at all in the original sense of 'to humour (a person)'. To humour someone in Chinese is to share a joke with them, one of the numerous examples of translation difficulties.

There are other Chinese attributes that stem, to some degree at least, from the nature of the language. Written Chinese imparts facts; you are told of situations, and advised of information, usually precisely, and an omission is assumed as such. You do not say 'yes we have no bananas'. You make it clear that the fruit is unobtainable. Descriptive passages can be repetitious, with the subject recurring, in a language which lacks a relative clause and thus has no direct equivalent of 'who' or 'which'.

This is not necessarily irksome to people who are accustomed to learning characters by rote. This also serves to propagandize, as in for example Mao's earlier works. These would, in simple language propound and repeat a theme, to be read and repeated and followed, such as how the force leading our cause is the Chinese Communist Party. Yet the lack of a formal grammar also makes for a contradictory fluidity, and spoken Chinese can on occasion be imprecise. So, for example, numbers can be vague, several tens, anything from 11 to 99 people, are present, and so on. Insults are carefully crafted and obliquely delivered. Well-known Chinese characteristics, such as the importance of face or appearance, do not of course stem directly from language; but manners dictate that if rebukes have to be imparted then this should be done obliquely, and bad news is told indirectly if possible. By the same token, *guanxi* or connections, the basis of many Chinese relationships which cut corners and oil the wheels, has a considerable vocabulary covering every relationship under the sun. This in turn harks back to the traditional Chinese extended family. Spoken Chinese, by its flexibility, also lends itself to the indirect approach where 'maybe' means 'never', and 'difficult' means 'no'. There are also numerous euphemisms; people do not die, they resign from the world; they also ascend to the hall of learning, go to your palace, invite you to their humble shack, and so on. With such a difficult and complex language, it is no surprise that learning is prized and a teacher highly respected. This has always been so, and there are many tales of dedicated teachers and gifted students. The many Chinese students nowadays abroad are particularly noted for their diligence and prowess at examinations.

At the time of the Communist take-over in China, over 50 years ago, it was generally considered rather eccentric and unusual for Westerners to learn the Chinese language, and very few did. One or two universities in Europe and North America offered Chinese language studies as a subject, in one instance classical Chinese only. There were few textbooks and dictionaries available, and none of the modern aids such as language laboratories. There was, however, no shortage of Chinese willing to teach their language among the growing tide of refugees that were flooding into HongKong. A few diplomats learned Mandarin, some colonial police officers in HongKong and Malaya learned Cantonese, there were some academics and of course a number of missionaries who had spent a lifetime in China. Of the mercantile community, resident or visiting, practically none spoke a word. In China a few officials spoke Russian, some English; in major centres such as Shanghai those who had been dealing with or working for Westerners before 1949 had good

English. Interpreters were always provided for all occasions, whether needed or not. Rigid state control, the bottleneck system of trade negotiation and the minimal contact with Chinese for foreigners in China made the difficult communication situation viable.

Since the Open Door, when China ceased her policy of self-reliance and opened up to foreign investment, trade and technology to dramatic effect, much has changed; far more Westerners are learning Chinese and far more establishments teach it. Yet to this day only a tiny fraction of the resident Western population in China speaks Chinese, let alone writes the characters. Chinese remains a difficult language and it is a full-time job to learn it. Chinese are still surprised when a Westerner speaks their language and are pleased that he or she has taken the trouble to do so.

5
Administering Wealth: Chinese Thinking About Economics

One of the most problematic issues for any businessperson in China today is the relationship between the state and the economy. In the West we have become used to thinking of the economy as something that gets along best when left on its own. The interests of both consumers and businesses are best served when government gets out of the way, or at least manages with only a light regulatory hand. Government involvement in business is seen as state interference in the economy. With exceptions, such as Marxism, most Western views have been along these lines; and with the fall of the Soviet Union, we have by and large convinced ourselves that our way is the only right one. So, when in China we see massive state interference in business and economics at almost every level, we tend to assume that this is wrong. It is, the theorists tell us, a holdover from Chinese communism, and will disappear when that system disappears (if it does, which is also a moot point).

It is quite true that under Mao, the Chinese economy was dominated by a modified form of communism. All economic power was gathered into the hands of the state, and all, or very nearly all, capital was nationalized. Companies were owned by the state and workers employed by it. As time passed, more and more property was nationalized or held communally, especially in country regions. While Western communism had stressed the role of the industrial proletariat, Maoism originally promoted the agricultural peasantry to a position of primacy. This was done for two reasons: the peasants needed to feel that they were at the centre of things if they were to be motivated to grow the food the country desperately needed, and Mao needed their vast numbers to recruit his armies to beat off the Japanese and overthrow the Nationalist government. Once in power, Mao and his administrators sought to achieve more of a balance between industry and agriculture, city and country.

Their entire economic outlook, however, was dominated by the need to increase production, and economic success was measured by the meeting of quota targets. When those targets were set unrealistically, as during the 'drive for steel' and the Great Leap Forward in the 1950s, the economy failed and mass starvation ensued.

Of all Mao's ideology, his economics were perhaps the most Western in origin. His ideas on social control were a blend of Confucianism and Legalism, but his economic thinking came with little modification straight from the Anglo–German–Russian communism of Marx, Kautsky and Lenin. When Mao was gone from the scene, and economic reforms began, people asked what kind of economic thinking would succeed it. Would China turn to capitalism, red in tooth and claw? Would a modified form of socialism prevail, such as the idea of the 'socialist market economy' touted by Deng Xiaoping and his successors (and widely ridiculed in the West)?

One feature that we are certainly likely to see continue is the government playing a strong and prominent role in guiding the economy. As the economic historian Gilbert Slater remarked a century ago, the boundary between economics and politics is everywhere difficult to define, but in China it is impossible to see a distinction. Under Mao, Deng and Jiang, that has remained as true as ever. The role of the state has certainly changed over the past quarter-century, but its presence remains strong. Also, the new direction that Chinese economic thinking seems to be taking, especially under Jiang Zemin and his successor, Hu Jintao, suggests that not much will change, at least in the minds of those in power. New-style Chinese economics is evolving away from communism, but it seems to be moving towards something that more nearly resembles the ideas of Confucius and his followers than it does anything we currently have in the West.

It is of course impossible to predict the future, but it seems entirely possible that the new Chinese economy could see the influence of ancient Chinese thinking about economics as well as modern capitalism and socialism. After all, those ideas guided the Chinese economy for several millennia, and it would be surprising if all their influence were to disappear overnight. And, as might be expected, there are several, sometimes contradictory, sets of ideas about economics to be found in Chinese thinking. The chief of these come from three of the great schools of Chinese philosophy, Confucianism, Taoism (Daoism) and Legalism. It is worth while taking a look at all three of these in order to get some idea of the influences that there have been, and may well continue to be, on the economy of China. Of course, how the economy develops determines the environment in which both Western and Chinese companies will operate and the problems their managers will face. In particular, it shows us the kinds of roles the government might play in economics and business in the future.

Confucian economics

Ancient Chinese contained no word for 'economics'; the modern term, *ching chi*, is a Japanese loanword and does not appear until the end of the nineteenth century. There is, however, a very ancient term, 'administering wealth', which appears in the *Book of Changes*, probably composed some time around 1000 BC, and later picked up and adopted by Confucius and many of his school. The idea of 'administering wealth' is central to what we might call 'Confucian economics', that is, Confucian ideas on the role that money, wealth and business play in society and their relationship to the state and government. A later scholar, Chen Huan-chang, a mandarin and reformer who went on to take a PhD at Columbia University in 1911 and whose *The Economic Principles of Confucius and His School* is still the best and clearest summary of Confucian thinking on this subject, suggested that 'administering wealth' is for all practical purposes the same as 'economics'.

'Administering wealth' is an interesting choice of term. Unlike in the West, where economic forces are sometimes seen as being like natural laws, the Confucians saw a direct link between economic activity and human agency. That is, what happened in the marketplace was determined directly by what people felt and what they did. The idea of the 'invisible hand' has no place at all in Confucian thinking. According to Confucius and his followers, there are three factors of production – land, capital and the virtuous man – and of these three it is the latter that is by far the most important.

Thus there is also a direct link between economics and ethics. The administering of wealth is not an end in itself; it is done for a purpose. In Confucian thought, wealth is inseparable from ethical and social considerations. The modern Confucian scholar A.S. Cua has referred to Confucianism as being at heart a system of ethics, and the Confucian approach to economics might almost be called an 'economics of virtue'. A quote from the *Great Learning*, one of the key texts of the golden age of Confucianism, sums this up:

> The superior man must be careful about his virtue first. Having virtue, there will be the man. Having the man, there will be the land.

> Having the land, there will be wealth. Having the wealth, there will be its use. Virtue is the root, and wealth is its only outcome.

At an individual level, we seek to earn money in order to give ourselves pleasure; we seek economic goals in order to derive pleasure for ourselves. Like the Reverend Thomas Robert Malthus 2,300 years later, Confucius saw the two overriding human needs as being for food and for sex. Others of his circle, notably Mencius and Xunzi, believed that things such as the need for personal honour and dignity also played a role. But whatever our needs may be, we seek to fulfil them, and the means we most commonly use is economic activity – making money.

This looks at first like an argument for the free market, but Confucius and his followers take the opposite tack. In order to remain virtuous, they say, economic activity must be managed and controlled. Controlling the economy is the task of sages and kings, whom Confucius advises to remain above or outside the economic system and act as external agents. He repeatedly says that those in positions of power should avoid personal enrichment, thereby having no personal stake in the economy's success.

Most notably, whereas Western economic theory usually argues that in order to achieve prosperity, supply should be increased in order to match demand, Confucius said instead that demand should be curbed so as to meet supply. He proposed not only economic controls (such as sumptuary laws to inhibit demand for luxuries) but also the curbing of human wants through moral and social education. By restricting demand to what the economy could produce, the evils of excessive competition could be avoided; it was only when demand outstripped supply that competition began and suppliers began exploiting people and overcharging them. But this restriction of demand did not necessarily mean that people should be poor. Himself a government minister in a north Chinese kingdom of the pre-empire period, Confucius was once asked what should be done for the betterment of the people. His answer was twofold: educate them, and make them wealthy. Education bred an understanding of the uses of wealth; wealth made possible the benefits of education, and both led to self-development.

Interestingly too, the Confucians rejected competition. This is particularly evident in the views of Mencius, which Dr Chen summarizes as follows:

> If we should ... let competition be absolutely free, the world would be left to the few strongest only. Although we cannot do very much

> against nature, how can we bear to see the sufferings of the weak, who constitute the greatest part of mankind? Therefore, no great religious teachers, nor great moralists, nor great statesmen, let nature alone without some sort of regulation. Since natural selection is good, not for the weak, but for the strong only, artificial adjustment for society as a whole is necessary.

This strong view led some in the modern period, Chen included, to speak of 'Confucian socialism', and Mao himself was known to speak highly at times of Confucius's views on this subject.

But at the same time as rejecting competition, however, the Confucians also rejected monopoly. They argue that everyone who wishes to engage in economic activity has a right to do so, and there should be no barriers to entry. The task of the market regulator (the state) is to prevent any one person from gaining advantage over the others. The means by which this is done is the matching of supply and demand, principally, as noted, by restraining demand. When supply and demand are perfectly balanced, then goods will be brought to market at a price which is fair to all buyers and to all sellers. Everyone will fulfil their economic aims of enhancing pleasure. Needless to say, this Confucian version of the 'perfect market' proved impossible to realize, but later Confucian scholars, in a way typical of scholars everywhere, blamed these failures on the execution of the projects themselves, and argued that their proponents did not follow Confucian doctrines closely enough.

Confucianism did have a strong economic core, and its guiding principles were in fact followed. If we look at the history of Chinese economics and society over the 2,000 years or so that followed Confucius, we can see that most of the above was actually put into practice. Individual businesses and business concerns did flourish in China. The Tongrentang pharmacy, still in operation today on Dazhalan in Beijing, had a nation-wide network of shops by the mid-eighteenth century and was a famous Chinese brand name. Caizhi Zhai, the famous Suzhou confectioners, were also a big business. But all operated under authority, usually twofold; the various craft and industrial guilds, which practised self-regulation and urged – in very Confucian style – members to cooperate for the good of all, rather than competing; and the state, which could and did intervene to control economic activity when it chose.

In the late nineteenth century, when China first came under the scrutiny of Western economists and political scientists, the latter argued that Confucianism was in some way 'anti-economic'; that is, it was prejudiced against business and assigned it little importance. By selectively quoting from some of Confucius's attacks on the immorality of the rich, men like the German sociologist Max Weber built up a picture of a Confucian system in which the ossified bureaucracy that ruled China was utterly opposed to progress and business expansion. Chinese scholars agree that the ossification occurred precisely *because* China's rulers had abandoned the true principles of Confucianism. Refomers like Kang Youwei, who tried to reform the imperial court before being forced into exile in 1898, attacked the education system which siphoned off the country's intellectual talent into the civil service, leaving agriculture and industry to make do with leavings and thus inhibiting innovation and creativity in those areas.

The aim of Confucianism, according to reformist scholars not only in the 1890s but for centuries before, was to build the perfect society. The ultimate aim of society is the Great Similarity, or Extreme Peace, a utopian vision in which all of mankind will be equal and conflict and poverty will not exist. Achieving the Great Similarity requires not only the cultivation of virtue, but also the cultivation of wealth. The Great Similiarity, when it is achieved, will include not only China but the whole world. All people in the world are interdependent economically, and all behave economically for the same reasons. Thus, two and a half millennia before Immanuel Wallerstein proposed the concept in the West, Confucius and his followers were groping towards the idea of an economic world-system, or globalization.

At the highest level, the Confucians linked economics to religious belief. Referring to the two primary needs mentioned above, Confucius believed that when people have enough to eat (and, presumably, enough sex), their minds can then begin to dwell on higher, spiritual things. As Dr Chen later commented 'economic satisfaction is the condition necessary for the development of religion.'

Taoism and *laissez-faire*

The Confucians of the late empire rejected the idea of *laissez-faire*, the free market economy in which the checks and balances of supply and demand always (well, nearly always) ensure that needs are met. There was an irony here, however, as *laissez-faire* is itself almost certainly Chinese in origin, and comes from the rival school of Taoism. As we mentioned in Chapter 3, one of the principles of Taoism is the belief that true achievement comes not through action but rather through its opposite, *wu-wei*, or 'non-action'. The Taoist view was that the most efficacious way of achieving a desired result is through stillness, causing things to happen without intervening. In economic terms, this means letting natural economic laws run their course.

The central Taoist text, the *Dao De Jing*, remains widely read in China, and the text is perceived as having important things to say about business culture and leadership. The book exhorts those in positions of power and authority to know much, but to do little. Chapter 8, for example, urges: 'In governing, know how to maintain order. In transacting business, know how to be efficient. In making a move, know how to choose the right moment.' Chapter 17 says that the most effective form of leadership is that which motivates people rather than controlling them:

> The highest type of rule is one of whose existence the people are barely aware.
> Next comes one whom they love and praise.
> Next comes one whom they fear.
> Next comes one whom they despise and defy.
> When you are lacking faith,
> Others will be unfaithful to you.
> The Sage is self-effacing and scanty of words.
> When his task is accomplished and things have been completed,
> All the people say, 'We ourselves have achieved it!'

The highest form of rule, says the *Dao De Jing*, is that which is conducted according to the principles of virtue and the Way; the lowest is that which is conducted according to ritual and ceremony, for these are 'the beginning of all confusion and disorder' (Chapter 38). Another important aspect is the emphasis on the intangible. This is highlighted in Chapter 11:

> Thirty spokes converge upon a single hub;
> It is on the hole in the centre that the use of the cart hinges.
> We make a vessel from a lump of clay;
> It is the empty space within the vessel that makes it useful.
> We make doors and windows for a room;
> But it is the empty spaces that make the room liveable.
> Thus, while the tangible has its advantages,
> It is the intangible that makes it useful.

The focus on the intangible leads to the concept of *wu-wei* or non-action, whereby the ruler does not do things; rather, he causes them to happen. In a society or organization which is focused on the Way, right things happen naturally and of their own accord without need for the ruler's intervention. The task of the latter, then, is solely to guide the organization along the Way and in accordance with the principles of virtue.

The principal ideas of Taoist thought had reached the West by the early eighteenth century, thanks to translations of its main works by Jesuit missionaries. These translations were then sent back to the West, especially France. There they became an important, though often overlooked, influence in the thinking of the eighteenth-century European Enlightenment. The school of economists known as the physiocrats, including such pioneers of modern economic thinking as Cantillon, Quesnay, Argentan and Turgot, were also influenced by these ideas. It was François Quesnay who first explored the idea of *wu-wei*, and we can see in his writing the deliberate adaptation of the Taoist concept to Western usage, to mean that things happened best when they happened naturally, of their own volition, rather than being compelled or forced to happen. In economic terms, Quesnay and his colleagues argued, the state was required to create conditions in which economic good would result naturally, rather than trying to lead or direct economic activity. They termed this principle *laissez-faire*. Although Adam Smith does not actually use the term *laissez-faire* in *The Wealth of Nations* (first published 1776), he was strongly influenced by the physiocrats, and he takes the concept of *wu-wei* a step further: he postulates that markets, if left unhindered by government intervention, will act naturally to do good and to distribute wealth where it is needed, the famous 'invisible hand'. Thus the founders of modern free-market capitalism drew one of their key ideas from a 2,000 year old Taoist concept.

Laissez-faire came full circle to China after the 1911 Revolution, when a succession of Republican governments attempted to set up a free market economy. The Republicans, and the Communists, quickly learned that a free market meant laying China open to foreign economic domination. It has made a second partial return since 1979. But there is a third approach to the management of economy which has also played a role, both under the empire and under Mao.

Power and control

Although as we said at the start of this chapter the heart of Mao's economic thinking was a modified version of Western communism, he had good words to say for Confucius as well. And it is possible to see in the Maoist economic system the influence of the third great early Chinese system of thinking, Legalism. As we noted in Chapter 3, Legalism was brought to its fullest extent by Han Feizi, the minister and ideologue who influenced the first emperor of unified China, Qin Shi Huangdi (221–206 BC). Han Feizi rejected the Confucian notion that most men tend towards the good and can be relied upon to behave ethically through a social system that exerts pressure on people to conform. To him, the only way to achieve conformity was through the rule of law.

Han Feizi's ideas are properly political rather than economic, but they have economic overtones. His thinking was based on three important principles. The first of these was *fa*, meaning roughly 'prescriptive standards', but also with connotations of law and punishment. People should comply with *fa* so that their behaviour conforms with the public good, or be punished as a result. The second was *shi*, meaning 'authority' or 'power'. The exercise of *shi* is necessary to ensure compliance with *fa*; but conversely, *shi* should also be governed by the dictates of *fa* to prevent abuses of power. The third was *shu*, the technique of controlling the bureaucracy by comparing 'word' with 'deed' (or more generally, potential performance with the actuality).

Taken together, the three principles of *fa, shi* and *shu* provided a system of management that was the guiding force for Chinese administration for the next two millennia, at least until the fall of the Empire in 1911. Nor does it take too much imagination to see the same influences under Mao. State economic planning assumed that the state knew what the public good was, and people who failed to work towards the good were punished; the state used its authority or power to ensure that the punishment was carried out. Finally, the target-setting of the Five-Year Plans is on the one hand straight Marxist-Leninism, but on the other hand has strong overtones of *shu*.

One habit of Chinese intellectuals, most of who detest confrontation and disagreement, is to try and seek consensus whenever possible. In the twelfth and thirteenth centuries, for example, when the competing belief systems of Confucianism, Taoism and Buddhism were at loggerheads, a group of thinkers led by the Cheng brothers and Zhu Xi worked out a compromise system which incorporated elements of all three, though with Confucianism taking the dominant role. This system, which Westerners sometimes called 'Neo-Confucianism', lasted until the fall of the empire. Today, with old-style Confucian thinking, capitalism (whether Taoist-inspired or not) and Legalist authoritarianism are present and prevalent in Chinese society, it seems inevitable that someone will try to work out a compromise that again incorporates all three; and don't be too surprised if Confucianism comes out on top again. The Chinese belief in state control and intervention of the economy long predates communism, and it is thus hardly logical to expect it to die with communism.

Is all this fanciful theory? In November 2002 at the Sixteenth Congress of the Communist Party of China, the Party adopted the 'three represents' philosophy, which had been spelled out earlier in the year by then-President Jiang Zemin. This is the idea that the Party (and by implication the government) should work to represent the interests of the growing Chinese economy, the development of Chinese culture, and the needs of the Chinese people. In other words, economic growth is one pillar of future Chinese development, but is linked to and inseparable from the social and cultural needs of the country and society at large. Another resolution at the same congress called for the rule of law to be combined with the rule of virtue, as Confucian an idea as one could ever wish to see.

We can think of no neater, more concise encapsulation of the three principles of Confucianism, capitalism and authoritarianism than Jiang's 'three represents'. And remember: this is the guiding philosophy of the men (and occasional woman) ruling China now, and will remain so for the next several years. Fanciful theory it may indeed be; but the people running China believe it, and they will expect Western business people, whom they still see as guests in their country, to conform to it.

6

Mutual Misunderstanding: Mandarins, Cadres, Taipans and Traders

An observer who visits China and has studied her past will note how the anxious debate over the placement for a dinner party attended by ranking Communist Party members demonstrates a Confucian view of hierarchy, that a kindly teacher may exude Mencius, and a clerk in the visa section of any Chinese embassy may be a Legalist. It is harder to define Taoism; someone once said it was best exemplified by watching three Chinese, of equal rank, inviting each other to pass through a swing door. More generalizations to be argued include the contention that in Chinese eyes there are five distinct categories of foreigner involved with China. First are the '*lao pengyou*/old friends', often businessmen who have a long and satisfactory relationship with the Chinese and who are liked, trusted and respected. The highest level they can reach is to become a Friend of China, and the Chinese will tell them when they have done so. Then, entirely different, there are the China watchers, a fairly large corpus of journalists, writers and academics who investigate and analyse the Chinese scene. Their standing in Chinese official eyes mainly relates to what they write and some are often unpopular. Previously, China watchers known to be hostile were not allowed into China, save for brief, carefully controlled visits; now they travel relatively freely.

Different again, but equally noteworthy, are what has been aptly called the China lovers, a fairly small band of dedicated men and women, past and present, who have given their all to China and the Chinese as revolutionary soldiers, or doctors, or teachers. These people hardly impinge at all upon the business world. The fourth type is rather a bad joke; those who practise what is here christened Chinesemanship. This consists of showing off a knowledge of things Chinese at every opportunity and in particular any knowledge of the language. Chinese present are invariably polite, and will even hail a request for a cup of tea by the Chineseman in bad Mandarin as a fluent command of the tongue. These people also often exhibit a tedious knowledge of archaic customs and, at dinners, the ingredients of what they are eating, welcoming each new dish with an obsolete toast. Chinesemen usually say that many of their best friends are Chinese; that is the hallmark of the true practitioner.

There are also diplomats, often an amalgam of the categories above; some are old friends, many are watchers for that in a different way is their job, very few are China lovers, fewer still are overt practitioners of Chinesemanship. The fifth, and by far the largest category, constitutes the Western businessmen who, in increasing numbers, and without too many pre-conceived notions, are coming to China to engage in business. Usually they are better informed than before; most have been well briefed, have attended courses, read books, studied background, consulted others. A few have even attempted the language and many have every intention of learning Chinese until they realize the extent of the commitment and the limited time available. Practically all are involved in business on a long-term basis; some despair or grow disenchanted, but have invested too much time and effort to give up. Most are active members of their country's China Business Association and share both advice and information with others. In time some too will become old friends, if they persevere, perhaps even Friends of China. They will get to know a market and a situation that is changing yet still full of surprises. Lastly there are also a few Old China hands, now a somewhat pejorative term, covering those who knew China long ago; other categories of foreigner previously found in China such as missionaries and mercenary soldiers have completely disappeared. All share a view of China that is slowly altering as China changes. The Chinese themselves are concerned this should be a good view and seem largely content to leave it to Westerners to explain and interpret China to each other. Chinese curiosity about the West tends to be more material than intellectual, with some exceptions such as academics, diplomats and other intellectuals; the Western approach varies and much remains in the eye of the beholders on both sides, who stick to preconceived notions and make little effort to improve their understanding.

The Western view of China was constant for a very long time. The early impression, largely by repute, was of a vast and fabulous country ruled over by a benevolent autocracy headed by a wise emperor to be admired from a distance and on rare occasion visited by adventurous explorers, and this more or less lasted until the eighteenth century.

Subsequent decline and obvious weakness, with the increasing inability to resist aggressive outside pressures, meant that many came to view China with little respect and had scant regard for her institutions. The merchants and adventurers came to plunder, the Western powers sent ships and troops to force concessions. The Chinese themselves were unable to do anything much to influence outside opinion. This state of affairs lasted through much of the nineteenth century and the first half of the twentieth century. Later when the Communists came, they stated their case to the world in unequivocal terms, usually on a take-it-or-leave-it basis. They expected anyone who dealt with China to accept without question their own evaluation. Meanwhile there had long been a series of standard views on China widely accepted at the time; so there had already grown up a popular image, fostered by certain Western writers, of delicate people with long fingernails and inscrutable expressions speaking in aphorisms, or coolies pulling rickshaws occupied by pot-bellied mandarins, all set against a background of willow pattern scenery. After 1949 there was a picture of oppressed peasants starving in vast labour camps, or diligent blue-coated ants ('Mao's blue hordes', as American propagandists liked to call them) swarming over huge construction sites. All these images, past and present, have often been encouraged by certain so-called China experts of various kinds in the West, who interposed their views of China on the world. Not so many Chinese have interpreted their country to the foreigner.

Long ago, the earliest travellers told of a great and civilized empire, with magnificent cities and a unique system of government and society. Tales to this effect filtered back along the Silk Road to Europe, over the mountain passes to India and via nomad tribes across the Siberian steppe to Muscovy. The most celebrated account was by the thirteenth-century Venetian, Marco Polo, probably China's best-known visitor ever. Later during the sixteenth and seventeenth centuries, a very small band of courageous and dedicated Jesuits following orders from Rome succeeded in establishing themselves in China and formed the first intellectual bridge with the West; scholars in their own right, they were the first to learn the language and understand the culture. The difficulties were well nigh insuperable; missionaries such as Ricci and Ruggieri learnt Chinese empirically by acting out a word, having a Chinese write the character with a brush, and noting down the sound phonetically. Their disappointment to find they had but been learning a coastal dialect as they travelled into the interior was acute. Others, Adam Schall and Verbiest, established an observatory and taught astronomy, and also other technical skills such as the casting of cannon. These men, and their followers, had a great respect for Chinese civilization; they may have tried to influence it by attempting the conversion of Chinese to Christianity with very limited success, but they recognized its intrinsic qualities. They in turn left a legacy of respect accorded to wise and erudite scholars who were able to bridge two different cultures.

Meanwhile, trade was starting to grow, chiefly Chinese exports to Europe of silk, tea, rhubarb and porcelain. In the eighteenth century these products became fashionable, and things Chinese caught on. The intelligentsia in London and Paris were intrigued and fascinated by this enormous country and its philosophy of government. Latin translations of the *Analects* of Confucius were available in Paris by 1687 and in 1756 Voltaire declared the highest achievement of the Chinese empire was 'morality and law'. This was a time when China had more impact on the West than the other way round, and the British emissary Macartney's despatches on his return from China at the very end of the century were a shrewd analysis of the true state of affairs. He, and others like him, inquisitive and acquisitive, saw it as their duty and their right to establish normal trading relations between China and the West. Lord Macartney set out from London on the long voyage to China in late 1792 with clear instructions. He was, first of all, to establish diplomatic relations and having done this, sign a treaty of commerce and friendship between Britain and China that would improve the conditions under which British merchants traded at Canton and also, if possible, open up new markets for British goods in the north. It was also hoped that a representative of the King of England would be allowed to take up permanent residence in Peking. To this end, Macartney brought with him an entourage of scientists, draughtsmen, painters, gardeners, botanists, engineers and serving military officers, carried in a 64-gun man-of-war and an East Indiaman, the largest and fastest of that famous company's fleet. On board were carried presents designed both to please the emperor and demonstrate British scientific knowledge and technical achievement.

When, after much delay, Macartney had an audience of Qian Long at his summer hunting palace at Jehol (northeast of Beijing), he was courteously received. The obvious superiority of British cannon on the formidable HMS *Lion*, which could have sunk the entire Manchu navy, the scientific instruments far in advance of anything yet seen in China, the ascent of the redoubtable Dr Dinwiddie in an air balloon over the roofs of the imperial palace and his dive in a diving bell in the Bei Hai lake, the air pumps, spring postchaises, etc., were of no interest at all to those at court, Manchu or Chinese, who saw them. Of the gifts Macartney brought there was some slight interest only in some rather pleasingly designed Wedgwood ware. Of his requests, there was never a shadow of hope that they be granted for the mission was doomed to failure before it started. There were those who thought British unwillingness to observe court ritual, in particular Macartney's refusal to *kow-tow* (entailing indicating submission by prostration and banging the head on the floor), had to do with the failure of the mission. Not at all, such lapses were merely put down as ignorance on the part of the barbarian who, it was noted, would soon be leaving anyway. What Macartney's mission did however achieve was to bring home a wealth of detail on China of the time with a realization that normal diplomacy would not work, though further attempts were to be made.

The edict handed down by Qian Long giving his reply to King George III is quoted in part, for it sums up the entire situation:

> We, by the Grace of Heaven, Emperor, instruct the King of England to take note of our charge.
>
> Although your country, O King, lies in the far oceans, yet inclining your heart towards civilization you have specially sent an envoy respectfully to present a state message, and sailing the seas he has come to our Court to *kow-tow* and to present congratulations for the Imperial birthday, and also to present local products, thereby showing your sincerity.
>
> We have perused the text of your state message and the wording expresses your earnestness. From it your sincere humility and obedience can clearly be seen. It is admirable and we fully approve…
>
> As to what you have requested in your message, O King, namely to be allowed to send one of your subjects to reside in the Celestial Empire to look after your country's trade, this does not conform to the Celestial Empire's ceremonial system, and definitely cannot be done… These are the fixed regulations of the Celestial Empire, and presumably you also know them… Why, then do foreign countries need to send someone to remain at the capital? This is a request for which there is no precedent and it definitely cannot be granted…
>
> Now you, O King, have presented various objects to the throne, and mindful of your loyalty in presenting offerings from afar, we have specially ordered the Yamen to receive them. In fact, the virtue and power of the Celestial dynasty has penetrated afar to the myriad kingdoms, which have come to render homage, and so all kinds of precious things from over the mountain and sea have been collected

> here, things which your chief envoy and others have seen for themselves. Nevertheless, we have never valued ingenious articles, nor do we have the slightest need of your country's manufacturers. Therefore, O King, as regards your request to send someone to remain at the capital, while it is not in harmony with the regulations of the Celestial Empire we also feel very much that it is of no advantage to your country. Hence we have issued these detailed instructions and have commanded your tribute envoys to return safely home. You, O King, should simply act in conformity with our wishes by strengthening your loyalty and swearing perpetual obedience so as to ensure that your country may share the blessing of peace.

Note the opening assumption that Macartney had really come all that way to bring birthday greetings. In his journal, Macartney gave a penetrating and incisive summary of the China he saw:

> The Empire of China is an old, crazy first rate man-of-war, which a fortunate succession of able and vigilant officers has contrived to keep afloat for these one hundred and fifty years past, and to overawe their neighbours merely by her bulk and appearance, but whenever an insufficient man happens to have the command upon deck, adieu to the discipline and safety of the ship. She may perhaps not sink outright; she may drift some time as a wreck, and will then be dashed to pieces on the shore; but she can never be rebuilt on the old bottom.

Rapid and easy victories by Western arms in the early and mid-nineteenth century then changed everything. Here was a prize, equal to India. There was a pioneer spirit among the earlier settlers in the first treaty ports, Canton, Xiamen (Amoy), Fuzhou, Ningbo and Shanghai, and by 1850 there were about 200 trading concerns dotted up and down the coast, the majority of them British with American, French and Scandinavians also involved. The Germans came later, and the Japanese not until the twentieth century as they modernized and grew to equal status with European powers. Japan had meanwhile defeated China in the Sino–Japanese War of 1895–6 and now controlled the Korean peninsula.

Since there were no facilities at all, the early merchants provided all their own services from housing to water supply. There were ship chandlers, insurance brokers, publishers with a couple of English language-newspapers in circulation, steamship agents, plus a scattering of clergymen, doctors, lawyers and the inevitable remittance men, mainly at Shanghai. The Treaty of Nanjing in 1842 opened up a halcyon period with Western commerce unchallenged and foreign chambers of commerce sponsored commercial expeditions that travelled far into the interior. Communication with Britain was by clipper, the voyage taking less than three months. There were also sailings across the Pacific to the American west coast. Later came steamships, with sailings from major European ports and the east coast of the United States; overland travel by train began at the end of the century.

Meanwhile the Chinese view on the West had also altered. The original concept was from a Middle Kingdom which had already existed for two millennia in splendid isolation and with such a conceit of itself that outside dealings on equal terms with any non-Chinese entity was, by definition, impossible. There were no equal states, only vassals, and the concept of an equal relationship with a remote country far away was unthinkable. Nearer to home there were vassal states such as Korea and Annam that sent annual tributes to the Emperor and were allowed to visit and trade, at set times, via set routes, supervised and regulated. Any contact implied a supplicant, and any relationship was a boon conferred. Round the Chinese borders the barbarian tribes were, with varying degrees of success, kept out and any transfer of technology to them was strictly forbidden. It was hoped some carefully supervised contact might teach them the benefits of Chinese civilization. With a few exceptions, Chinese were forbidden to travel abroad and later, to have any intercourse with foreigners, even to teach them Chinese, which at times was proscribed on pain of death. A very small foreign residential presence was first accepted at the Han and Tang courts; later in the thirteenth century there was an enclave at Zaiton for Arab traders; Jesuit fathers lived and worked at the Ming court, later still and under pressure, Europeans came to Canton during the eighteenth and nineteenth centuries. This ghetto grew larger and stronger as the empire decayed, becoming, together with Western demands for relations on equal terms, the *cause celèbre* of the Opium War and further foreign encroachment. By then things were already going downhill.

As Chinese thinking stagnated, so the more outward looking and innovative approach of the early great dynasties had by the eighteenth century degenerated into what was at times an almost wilful ignorance of the outside world on the part of the court. Emperor and ministers were, for example, totally oblivious of the importance of China's growing foreign trade and Chinese settlements overseas. Indeed, the view of anything not readily understandable or unpleasant, or that did not fit into the scheme of things, was to deny its existence. Quite staggering misconceptions of the West existed; that Portugal lay to the south of Java, having previously been a Buddhist country before conversion to Catholicism, that descriptions of the five continents were untrue, and so forth. These were largely due to lack of contact and communication, plus imagination fuelled by traditional concepts and mythologies. The whole was compounded by arbitrary and varying transliterations of European names into Chinese, which caused great confusion, and the almost total inability of either side to speak each other's language, with the very limited vehicle of pidgin English as the sole medium of communication. The officials who dealt with Westerners, with a few notable exceptions who were able for a time to stop the rot and stem the tide, were venal and ritualistic, quite unable to cope, dealing in shadow rather than in substance, yet regarding Westerners with well-founded apprehension and mistrust. Indeed it is said that when the question of ceding HongKong to Britain was discussed at court, no one could find it on the map.

These people lived in a hidebound and increasingly moribund Confucian state, by now in an advanced state of decay, that had the misfortune to come up against an aggressive West seeking markets. China never had a chance, and the humiliation all this brought about, compounded by rage and frustration at a supine and corrupt leadership, which might have done so much better, made for an underlying resentment and bitterness in attitude, traces of which remain to this day. The official Chinese approach was still one of refusing to face facts, but some of her abler officials learned how to deal with the foreigner, how to maintain a position despite holding a weak hand. In practical terms this meant learning foreign ways and attitudes, and on occasion using foreign expertise to serve China. Starting in the mid-nineteenth century a succession of able Westerners served the Manchu court with distinction. There was Charles Gordon, who commanded the Ever-Victorious Army and played a major role in suppressing the Taiping rebellion; Robert Hart who founded, among other things, the Chinese customs service; scholars such as James Legge who interpreted the Chinese classics to the West. Such men, and a few others, allied with some able Chinese statesmen, were able to help rally the empire to delay final collapse by quite a few years. Interestingly, the notable Westerners who helped China during these years mostly spoke no Chinese, but had an understanding of the people they dealt with. Likewise the Chinese generals and statesmen they helped knew no English, but were shrewd judges of character. All were realists.

Meanwhile, greatly increased contact had a rapid effect on the idealized Western views of the preceding century. The hard-bitten sea captains and traders who ventured to Canton and up the coast saw only a vast market, crumbling administration and venal officials. Bribery and force were the methods they used, and the opium trade flourished and grew. Accounts of the time tell how practically none of them spoke any Chinese at all, or were the slightest bit interested in anything but commerce. The sailors, riotously drunk on rum and red pepper in the stews of Hog Lane in Canton, viewed the local population with fear and contempt. The administrators who dealt with the authorities were baffled and frustrated. The missionaries saw souls to be saved, even by free meals if necessary. Living spartan lives, they were the only foreigners to speak Chinese. The merchants all lived in great style, with large houses set in compounds of two or three acres, including the offices and warehouses. Young bachelors out from home lived in a separate mess and dined regularly with the *taipan* or boss. All were looked after by innumerable servants, invariably addressed as boy, and lived what was called the life of Riley, oblivious to the mainstream of Chinese life around them. Those who survived the health hazards, the climate, the gargantuan meals and the heavy drinking were extremely well paid. In time what came to be known as the Shanghai mind developed; a view of China both cynical and disillusioned. As one said, 'commerce was the beginning, the middle and the end of our life in China – if there were no trade, not a man, except missionaries, would have come here at all.'

This sorry tale of Chinese decline continued, with worse to follow. Naïve attempts somehow to harness Western techniques but not embrace Western ways in the last years of the Qing dynasty failed. A younger generation, fired by patriotism, poorly organized, incompetent, brave, tried to save the day. The West did virtually nothing to help. There was meanwhile the example of Japan, which had come to terms with the situation *vis-à-vis* the West and was strong. Why could not China do the same? But the number of treaty ports or concessions increased apace; foreign interests ran what little industry there was, controlled the banking system, ran the customs; in short, much of the country's external economy was in the hands of Westerners, who regarded the government of the day with ill-concealed contempt, interspersed with alarm as a warlord drew near or civil war broke out anew, yet secure in the knowledge that Western force of arms was there to bail them out if need arose. These people came to China to make money and for no other reason whatsoever. And so this situation continued, through war and upheaval, right up to 1949. When other countries in

Asia were colonized by the West, there was sometimes a very limited form of *quid pro quo*; the Westerner came, took, made money, but invested in infrastructure, introduced efficient administration, encouraged local agriculture, even some industry. But in the case of China nothing was put back and so China was the loser, hands down, principally because she was not a colony and thus not viewed as a long-term capital investment.

By the eve of World War II the general attitude to China, with the obvious and notable exception of Japan by now gearing up to war, was a little more understanding and less arrogant than that of the previous century. There was sympathy, if little else, for China's stand against the Japanese in 1937 and aid, mostly private, started to be given in increasing quantity, principally by the United States. The American view on China was different. The Americans played no part in the scramble for concessions on the China coast at the end of the nineteenth century. They did however send a force to join the Eight Nation Army that landed at Tianjin in 1900 and marched inland to raise the siege of the Peking Legation quarter under Boxer attack. It was an American who organized the first group of Chinese students to study abroad, and certain American universities sponsored these visits. Missionaries and doctors worked mostly selflessly among poor Chinese and often under harsh conditions. There were also American-backed schemes for industrial and agricultural development, schemes that largely foundered on ineffective Chinese officialdom. Later, after the attack by Japan in 1937, a team of American volunteers known as the 'Flying Tigers' flew with the Chinese airforce and American reporters such as Edgar Snow and Theodore White were foremost in telling the world what was going on. Later, when America entered the war there was massive official support for China, military, economic and financial. This continued as support for the Nationalist government during the renewed civil war against the Communists after Japan's surrender. China's leader, Chiang Kai-shek, a Methodist whose wife spoke perfect English, was viewed as having the same aims and ideals as Americans. The United States view of China was paternalistic and proprietorial in the light of her massive and increasing commitment to Nationalist China. When the Nationalists were finally defeated in 1949, it was said by many that America had lost China, though it was never hers to lose. A curtain of hostility and incomprehension came down between the two nations.

In the main, however, the general Western approach around at this time was still rather condescending. Chinese were popularly regarded as rather quaint people who did everything back to front. Chinese books started at the back, they wrote up and down, right to left, wore white for mourning, women wore trousers and men wore gowns, the last name came first. Victorian writers had portrayed them as sinister, opium-smoking figures, and that is how Doré drew them at the time of his famous illustrations of the London poor. Brett Harte had painted a more sympathetic picture in his tales of California in the 1850s; others showed them as coolies, crammed in the hold of sailing ships. Then the image changed, thanks to authors such as Pearl Buck, who portrayed people with names such as Little Plum Blossom, Third Aunt or Fourth Cousin. Then there was the horrible Dr Fu Man Chu and the nice Charlie Chan to show that Chinese could be good detectives, and Judge Dee with his wisdom. It was generally accepted that Chinese were wise and indeed so-called Chinese proverbs were regularly inserted in Christmas crackers. Remarks were prefaced by 'Confucius, he say…' An old music hall song was entitled Ching Ching Chinaman, and there was Widow Twankey and Aladdin with his wonderful lamp. For occupation, the Chinese were said to be cooks and laundrymen. They existed on a diet of fried rice and sweet and sour pork. A term of opprobrium was to say that something was organized like the Chinese navy. The army could not march in step. It took a war and a revolution to change all this.

Meanwhile during this same period the Chinese had got to know better, and mostly dislike, the foreigner. Apart from obviously resenting the arrogance and ostentatious wealth to be seen in the Treaty Ports, there was indignation at foreign interference in Chinese international politics. The famous May 4 movement in Peking in 1919 was the first ever massive protest in the streets by students against a Western decision affecting China (the award of territory to Japan). Earlier, there had been remarks by Western politicians that 'the affairs of China are settled in Europe' and Western virtual domination of China's external trade was the subject of strikes and protest. Chinese intellectuals also found some Western commentary on local creeds and customs patronizing. The turn-of-the-century Boxer rising was a crude expression of nationalism, in part directed at Westerners in general, in particular foreign missionaries and their Chinese converts who were deemed 'false foreigners'. On the other side of the coin, far more Chinese had travelled abroad and knew English and were able to appreciate the great writers and thinkers of Western literature and some of the ideas of Western governments and society. Such knowledge sometimes resulted in frustration at China's plight. A few got to know Western intellectuals, who in turn visited China. On this level, both sides were increasingly better informed about each other. Western authors wrote more about China, often novels about European society capers in the concessions, but sometimes more seriously.

Living in the foreign concession areas of the treaty ports, the pre-war resident foreign businessman led a most comfortable existence, insulated from the Chinese around them. There was racing, polo, picnics and dinners; all the advantages and privileges of the colonial lifestyle as enjoyed by his predecessors but with far better health and security. Each national concession in the Shanghai International Settlement flew its own flag, had its own European officered police force, its own detachment of volunteer troops and, on occasion, the support of a garrison of regular troops. Gunboats lay off the waterfront or Bund, or upriver, and out to sea the various navies patrolled the China station. Managers, aided by young clerks sent out from home, were skilfully served by established Chinese compradores who dealt with the Chinese side of any transaction, acting as intermediaries between two sides who did not know how to deal with each other. Foreign enclaves, self-regulating and at arm's length from the mass of Chinese, dealing with or through designated intermediaries, were not of course a new phenomenon. What was different was where the power lay; at the very beginning they were in China on sufferance, for a long time since the visitors were calling the tune. These halcyon days ended with the outbreak of war; there was a short-lived revival of the good times for a few after 1945, when Japan surrendered and the war was over, and foreign business interests moved back into Shanghai and a few other ports. However, this was cut short by the Communist victory in 1949 when all these privileges came to an abrupt end. In the 1930s two-thirds of China's external trade was in foreign hands. Some of the resident businessmen trusted this state of affairs would continue for ever, but the more perceptive knew it never could since it was rotten and relied on Chinese weakness.

By 1951, Communist expropriation of all foreign investment without compensation was complete. The trading houses and banks had either closed down completely or were obliged to remain open and pay salaries to Chinese staff, but without conducting business. Practically all foreign businessmen had left, apart from a luckless few denied exit permits, pending settlement of claims against their firms. Missionaries too had been expelled or, in a few instances, languished in prison on trumped up charges of spying or subversion. Control was now entirely Chinese; the balance of commercial control had altered, and with it the Western view. Many were now rather frightened of the new China which was regarded as a bogeyman, particularly in the United States. Doing business in the years immediately following the establishment of the People's Republic of China in 1949 implied a certain political commitment. The United States was, for a start, unremittingly hostile and all commercial relations with China were proscribed by Congress. Some European countries recognized the People's Republic but looked askance at resuming any trade, and Western business with China largely ceased. Yet tenuous contact continued and by 1952 a small but growing business was evident in Western Europe. The rules were now different; a small number of specialized trading houses acceptable to the Chinese, many with political affiliations, handled most foreign trade with China. Every Western businessman who traded with China in the early 1950s had at least outwardly to acquiesce in the new aims of the People's Republic, and going to China was seen by some as a political act.

These China traders were professionals. They mostly knew little of Chinese history or culture and, with one or two exceptions, not a word of the language. If need be, they usually would, whatever their private views, readily agree with their hosts on everything and some even joined in the singing of revolutionary songs. It was believed that failure to act in this way might harm business prospects and the Chinese certainly never troubled to challenge this view. More usually, it seemed only to encourage the Chinese to believe their own propaganda. This sort of behaviour also applied to visiting groups of manufacturers and engineers, in China for the first time, taking part in an exhibition or technical seminar, who would take their cue accordingly. Most visitors who described China were euphoric in their praise. The Chinese regarded this as just and appropriate, believing not without reason that the West had treated China badly in the past, and it was time to redress the balance. The shambles and brutality of the later Cultural Revolution were also extolled by certain Western left-wing writers and academics who preached Chinese propaganda abroad, and were allowed relatively free access to China. On the whole visitors accepted China at her own valuation and were deferential in discussion, falling in readily with their hosts' way of talking and soon finding themselves referring to 'friends' rather than to 'people' and endlessly toasting friendship and collaboration. There are some who still do. At the same time, there was genuine and widespread sympathy for Chinese efforts at reconstruction, and admiration for the often selfless, dedicated and hardworking officials with whom visitors come in contact. Old China hands were also amazed at the cleanliness of the new China, the elimination of corruption, sweated labour, prostitution, opium smoking, all the old evils.

Certain experienced journalists, some of who had been bitterly hostile to the regime, changed their views with almost Pauline speed when they reached China, and it became fashionable to be converted.

Those who do business with China today are far better informed, and have access to copious background data and information from the Chinese themselves. In time many come to share a jaundiced view of the difficulties and delays all too often encountered, yet often get to like the people with whom they are dealing. In some cases business people who lack the resources for frequent visits to China and lengthy meetings consider giving up, but few do. This is partly because they have already invested too much effort and money; also of course, things can always change and get better. It is wise to double all estimates, of time, effort and expense nevertheless. Of course, misconceptions remain and sometimes there is a tendency to read more into Chinese attitudes and statements. It is often hard to establish with whom to deal, and generally very difficult to find out just what happened. The average Western businessman engaged in negotiations probably spends more time thinking about his Chinese counterparts than they do of him. Some visitors still sometimes feel at a disadvantage and come as the supplicant, thanking their hosts for allowing them to visit China in the first place, spend all their money, stay such a long time, come back again later. Until a very few years ago a curious change seemed to come over quite hard-headed businessmen when they went to China; temporarily, at least, they lost their critical faculties, acquiescing readily to their hosts' views, though not necessarily so readily to their business proposals. Seldom did they criticize any shortcomings. However, this generally sycophantic approach is ending as China ceases to be so mysterious and becomes (outwardly) a little more familiar.

In the years following the death of Mao, foreign business opinion tended to swing from optimism to pessimism and back again, usually in direct response to fluctuations in Chinese policy. In the heady days of 1978–9 when, for the first time, China opened her doors wider, and vast schemes were afoot, a certain euphoria prevailed, particularly among American businessmen who were new to the game. There were those who assumed a Letter of Intent to be a binding contract, who mistook cautious Chinese approbation of a project's possibilities to be the same as official endorsement, and so on. Quick results were expected. China's vast population once again caused people to dream of huge deals; the fundamental misconception of the size of the market being directly dictated by the size of the population arose, and indeed still exists. When it became rapidly apparent that much of this optimism was unfounded in the first instance, and when the Chinese realized that they too had been far too ambitious and started cutting back on the scale and the extent of the announced buying programme, there was a rapid reaction. Excessive optimism and overestimation of possibilities on both sides gave way to pessimism. Since then, the general view has been more balanced and in recent years China's fiscal and economic policies, supportive attitude to Asian problems and generally responsive stance has created confidence.

The Open Door Policy certainly affected one field of China business: promotion. New policies and the possibility of greatly increased sales led to a rapid increase in industrial and technical exhibitions, and an exaggerated impression of the market for Western consumer goods resulted in a lot of extremely expensive advertising. Abroad, numerous conferences explaining how to do business with China were set up; as with all meetings about China, they were very largely organized by and attended by non-Chinese. It also meant that some charlatans could flourish and a few bogus consultants succeeded in being retained by manufacturers trying to break into the market. Some exhibition organizers also pretended a need or interest in technology or equipment on the part of an area which existed in only the vaguest terms; they were initially well supported by manufacturers mesmerized by the size of the China market, whose naïve hopes were encouraged by skilful and cynical sales talk. There were also some publications claiming a penetration and a readership among end users that was pure conjecture; as in the case of the exhibitions, they flourished briefly as a result of skilful manipulation of Western hopes for business. In some cases claims were made in the name of China and the Chinese that were not gainsaid, probably because they were not even known about. Indeed, certain Chinese officials had their photographs and names printed in Western promotional brochures without their knowledge. This wave of what can only be described as China carpet-baggers did well in the few years after the new policies were announced in 1978–9. None of them emanated from China, but rather from Western trading partners and of course HongKong; all have long since been discredited.

China is now more open and accessible than ever before during her long history. Her people are, by and large, better off, the economy is stable and the rate of growth remarkable. Her relations with the rest of the world are constructive and China plays a definite role in international affairs. It is remarkable to think that all this has come about relatively recently; it was only a generation ago that Mao died after years of strife and turmoil. China has definitely changed, it is easier to communicate and do business, people are more open and better informed, on the whole there is goodwill to the foreign visitor. It is tempting, therefore, to think of a wholly modern China in tune with everywhere else, where much is new and the recent past an aberration. But thousands of years of eventful history and tradition cannot be denied; the old remains, both good and bad, sometimes modified, sometimes cloaked. There are still human rights abuses, and the prospect of plural democracy remains far off. Chinese do not discuss the former with Western visitors as they are both circumspect and embarrassed by such matters. A few might mention democracy; some will quote the vast and unstoppable flow of information coming into China which means the people are better equipped to make sensible decisions. It follows, therefore, that they are unlikely to engage in foolish activities as in the past. This rather neat reasoning is on a par with the oft-quoted dictum of taking what is good from the past, leaving what is bad. Chinese will of course listen politely to visitor's views and respond appropriately.

There is no doubt that the misunderstandings of former years have lessened greatly and both sides get on better than before. This is chiefly because they know much more about each other, including acceptance of the profound cultural differences that remain, and make allowances accordingly. However, it is still easy to go wrong.

7
China Stands Up: The Rise of Modern China

The first major humiliation China suffered at the hands of the West could well be taken as the starting point for the rise of modern China. This rise has been both confused and lengthy, beset with setbacks, bedevilled by internal dissension and a source of intermittent great suffering for the Chinese people. It has now been accomplished and it may be postulated that modern China, part of the world community, united, stable and developing, albeit with some mighty problems yet to be solved, more or less came of age when Deng Xiaoping initiated his far-reaching and dramatic Open Door policy in 1978. It can equally be argued that this long process began in 1842 when a weak and inept Manchu government signed the Treaty of Nanjing with Britain, ceding HongKong island, allowing foreign interests to trade and subsequently missionaries to proselytize. These cut-off dates at either end can only be arbitrary, they roughly encompass a process that one way and another has taken nearly a century and a half. Indeed, one can assume an earlier or a later date for the beginning of the process; its completion is now a *fait accompli*. China and her people are today bent upon growth and prosperity; the bitterness of the past is of course remembered but mentioned less than before.

The China of 1842 had a population of over four hundred million, mostly concentrated in the eastern provinces. There was considerable industry but no mechanization; mining, iron smelting, metal working, ship building, potteries, textiles occupied only a fraction of the population, the remainder of whom were peasants working the land, grouped by family and clan in thousands of villages, planting and harvesting crops that varied with the region. There was also a myriad of small local townships and a few great cities, self-sufficient and locally self-governing, ruled by local magistrates and scholar gentry, in turn responsible hierarchically to the provincial Viceroy and eventually to the Son of Heaven in Peking. The standard of living, health and education was low, though no worse than that of Europe of the time; people were illiterate, ignorant and superstitious; medical care if any was primitive, in time of periodic famine people starved, in time of flood they drowned. But when there were no natural disasters, or marauding bandits, or outbreaks of plague, life was secure and unhurried. It had been like that for hundreds of years; but a growing decline in public services and increasing corruption of officials meant that less was being done to repair the great works such as dykes on the Yellow River or the banks of the Grand Canal. Increased inter-provincial smuggling, principally of salt, affected revenue and the network of highways and waterways that traversed the country became increasingly unsafe. Lack of effective management meant that when crops failed, one province had plenty while the next one starved.

Some of the senior officials at court and in the provinces were aware of these problems, as they were of the growing opium trade and its baleful effects. By the early nineteenth century, opium from India, carried in British ships, was China's principal import, costing an increasingly large amount of China's silver reserve. The men who administered China were educated in the classics and many were of ability, though stultified in their efforts at reform by supine rulers surrounded by scheming and corrupt eunuchs trained from an early age to be attendants at court and wielding considerable influence. With a few exceptions they were victims of centuries of growing intellectual stagnation which made it difficult for a new idea to be understood, let alone acted upon. That China had never had a Renaissance and had not progressed intellectually for hundreds of years made it difficult to accept or adapt to change. The only big difference at the top was that the Manchus, including the Emperor himself, the dynasty from the North East, Manchuria, whose horsemen had conquered all China in the seventeenth century, now all spoke and wrote Chinese as their first language; they and their followers, including the huge army, were sinicized, although this did not prevent many Manchus from being killed by Han Chinese after the 1911 Revolution. Manchu troops were known as bannermen, from their tribal origins, and constituted regular soldiers serving for long terms and stationed in towns. Some were still the fierce warriors of 200 years before, but many were ill-disciplined, opium-smoking loungers who did nothing; on rare inspections, their officers would seek to swell the ranks to falsify the muster roll and thus draw more money. Uniform, equipment and drill were hundreds of years out of date; the drill book laid down that the first manoeuvre on encountering the enemy was to strike fear in his heart by executing a somersault and a shout. There was a navy, largely used to ward off pirates and patrol the coast; huge junks with lateen sails and compasses originally far in advance of those in the West, now long since outdated.

Western pressure and influence increased as the century progressed. The second Anglo–Chinese War, again basically about the foreign right to trade, ended finally with the Convention of Peking in 1860 after a British and French force sacked the Summer Palace in Peking and the court fled. Kowloon, the mainland opposite HongKong, was ceded to Britain and Western business was now firmly established up and down the coast in concessions, mostly known as Treaty Ports. These enclaves were self-administered and not subject to Chinese jurisdiction, an arrangement which suited both the Chinese government, which wished to insulate its people from Western influence, and of course the Western governments whose merchants could do virtually as they pleased in the pursuit of profit. The concept was known as extraterritoriality. There was also the Most Favoured Nation Clause; as each foreign power wrested a concession from the Chinese, so it was applied equally to the others. By now several hundred firms enjoyed these privileges, and more were to come and more concessions were made. These firms handled a large proportion of China's still relatively small external business. In time Western governments began to forego these concessions and the system was reduced much later in the 1920s and 1930s, finally abolished in 1943 when the last Treaty Port was handed back to China, by now a wartime ally against Japan. The European businessmen and their families who lived in these places spoke no Chinese, knew nothing of China and were there solely to make money. The only exceptions to this rule were the missionaries, many living frugal lives in the interior.

Meanwhile, a massive rebellion fuelled by social unrest and religion broke out in central China. This lasted 14 years and killed twenty million people. The Taiping Rebellion was put down with great difficulty principally by the able General Zeng Guofan with some Western assistance, especially from General Charles 'Chinese' Gordon and others who led the Western trained and equipped Ever-Victorious Army to victory. This weakened the government still further, particularly as the rebels were able to march north nearly to Peking. Its leaders were fanatical visionaries who preached a distorted Christianity with egalitarian overtones. China had not long recovered from this great blow when the Western drive for power and influence intensified; indeed, some observers started speculating that China could not continue for long as an independent state. The French expeditionary force involved in conquering Annam, still a vassal state, later to be part of French Indo-China, was checked on its advance by a Chinese army in 1885, about the only time Chinese arms ever prevailed against the West. The news of the victory took so long to reach Peking that a treaty had already been signed, making further concessions. The grab for China continued on the part of the major European powers, Britain, Italy, Germany and Russia, and the term 'cutting up the Chinese melon' became current; it was also said that 'the affairs of the China are settled in Europe.' Yet, paradoxically, China was viewed by some as a threat, the 'Yellow peril' a figment of imagination of the German Kaiser, who was possibly referring to Napoleon's earlier remark about the sleeping giant, China, who would one day awake. It was all a far cry from mid-eighteenth-century Paris where Voltaire extolled Chinese wisdom in government and the *Analects* were read by some of the intelligentsia.

The Boxers were so-called by Europeans as they practised traditional Chinese boxing, a stylized exercise still current today. Their rebellion in 1899–1900 nearly put paid to the dynasty once and for all. Fanatical peasantry in North China, angered at missionary activities and inflamed by rumours of Christian maltreatment of Chinese children, launched a campaign of slaughter throughout the region, killing not only Western priests, ministers and nuns but also Chinese converts to Christianity. Believing they had magical powers and were immune to the bullets of the government troops sent against them the Boxers carried all before them, investing Peking where the foreign community withstood a long siege in the Legation quarter. An allied force of troops from eight nations landed at Tianjin and marched inland, defeating a mediaevally armed army on the way, raised the siege and occupied the capital. As had happened 40 years before in the Anglo–Chinese war, the court fled, to return over a year later. Official Manchu policy had deplored the Boxers, some of whom disliked the alien dynasty anyway, though rumour had it the Dowager Empress, Cixi, otherwise known as the Old Buddha had abetted them; later she showed her feelings by supporting them openly in a public statement. This strong-willed woman had dominated the court for years. Originally an emperor's concubine, she had blocked or stifled every attempt at reform, prevailing over weak but well-meaning emperors and sincere but naïve reformers. Inevitably China had to make a grovelling apology and pay a huge indemnity it could ill afford.

There had been other disasters as the century ended. A resurgent and aggressive Japan, with a modern army and navy, challenged Chinese superiority over the vassal state of Korea, defeating a Chinese army sent to oppose them that was armed largely with spears and bows and arrows. By the Treaty of Shimonesiki in 1894 Korea became an independent kingdom, thus passing under Japanese influence. The island of Taiwan was also ceded. A few years later Japan defeated Czarist Russia at Port Arthur and also sank a large portion of the Russian navy; Japanese interests, backed by the military, encroached upon the Liaodong peninsula in Manchuria, a harbinger of much worse to come. There had also been rebellions against Manchu rule in the far West, non-Han areas peopled by Muslim tribesmen. But here the problem was dealt with intelligently and what was later called 'the agricultural army' led by Zuo Zongtang moved west, a slow advance as it planted and harvested on the way, so feeding itself and the people, and thus slowly pacified the region. Meanwhile, rather late due to official opposition, railways had come to China; during the so-called Battle of the Concessions, China gave Russia the right to build a strategic railway right across Chinese territory in Manchuria in 1896, and further similar concessions went to the British in the Yangzi valley, in Shandong to the Germans and the main Peking–Hankou line was built by Belgians. France was granted the port of Guangzhouwan in the south, the Germans got Qingdao in Shandong, the British Weihaiwei in the same province and the hinterland of the Kowloon peninsula, the New Territories, in HongKong.

It was amazing how China survived all this and yet remained a sovereign state. Part of the reason was that the vast Chinese hinterland was almost entirely unaffected by these foreign incursions which only occurred along the seaboard and up the great rivers. There had also occurred what has been aptly termed 'the last stand of Chinese conservatism', a concerted attempt by a group of able and conscientious officials devoted to their country and culture to stop the rot, preserve old values yet ensure China could keep abreast of a changing world. There was no thought of Westernization of industry, business, government or military as had happened in Japan, rather the application of Confucian ideas in a framework that had already lasted for over 2,000 years. Men such as Zeng Guofan, who had defeated the Taiping, and his successor Li Hongzhang, statesman and soldier, also proposed an overhaul of government structure and the introduction of an elite class partly educated on Western lines. They established arsenals and shipyards, Chinese owned and managed, near Shanghai and the first batch of pigtailed and long-gowned students left for America. But it was not enough, and by the 1890s a move was afoot for more radical reform, almost certainly doomed from the outset as it impractically proposed adopting Western practice within an essentially Chinese framework. In 1898, the young Emperor sanctioned what became later known as the Hundred Days reform, embracing the modernization of the imperial examination system, reform of the army and changes in government structure, but all was scuppered by the arch-conservative and powerful Dowager Empress Cixi, still the power behind the throne in every way. Noted reformers of the time, men such as Kang Youwei and Liang Qichao, attracted foreign sympathy but little in the way of support. Any change would have to come from within. It finally did, from the court itself in 1905, well after the Boxer disaster, but it was too late and the monarchy was already doomed.

There was another body of men who realized China's only hope lay in getting rid of the dynasty and forming a republic. These revolutionaries did not believe in reform but in revolution; they were gradually subsumed into the Tungmeng hui, later the Guomindang or Nationalist Party with the visionary Dr Sun Yat-Sen as its leader, by 1905. Sun was a Cantonese, educated abroad, a Christian and a fluent English speaker who pursued both his career as a doctor and his revolutionary activities outside China. He had nothing in common with the reforming Mandarins in Peking and was often on the run, trying to organize opposition; it was a difficult task as people were apathetic, and even those who hated the Manchu rule were not necessarily prepared to take risks. There was also an organized revolutionary underground, which struck after an accidental bomb explosion in Hankou; unrest spread and the garrison at nearby Wuchang on the Yangzi then mutinied. The revolt gathered force; there was some resistance, but not for long and the widespread discontent of young educated Chinese became felt. At the same time many Han army units turned against the Qing rulers, who rapidly lost control. This was 10 October 1911, and the so-called Double Tenth, one of the most famous dates in Chinese history. Sun was travelling in Canada when the coded cable arrived with the news and it took a further three days before he could find the key and read the contents and several weeks before he got back to China. It was soon arranged to save face that court and emperor, stripped of all power, were allowed to continue to reside in imperial splendour in the Forbidden City in Peking. Meanwhile the Republic of China was proclaimed amid rejoicing by Chinese intellectuals and reformers, indifference by most. A national assembly was formed and the first election gave victory to the Guomindang.

The new republican government, complete with democratic constitution based on Dr Sun's three principles of nationalism, democracy and people's livelihood, set to work with a will but achieved little. Good relations with the West were sought, albeit with considerable resentment at the way foreign interests had dominated the economy for so long, such as imposing commodities and crops which supplanted native products. Thus tobacco farming was introduced along parts of the north east seaboard and in central China, with the leaf bought very cheaply from peasants who had no one else to sell it to. Likewise there was a monopoly on the supply of domestic fuel throughout much of China, and Chinese industry was largely dominated by foreign capital using cheap local labour. Textiles, milling, canning and similar light industry grew up in Shanghai, Tianjin, Hankou and at major railway intersections, which in time caused an increasing drift of peasants to the towns and so the creation of an urban working class, more politically conscious and no longer so closely bound by tradition. Western interests also largely ran the country's external banking system, such as it was, and some official institutions, including the customs service and port inspectorate, right up until the early 1930s. Established business houses, based mostly in Shanghai, the chief commercial centre, with branches in other treaty port towns, ran a network of distributors in the interior which assured a continued flow of consumer imports from abroad along the eastern seaboard. Tariffs remained low and there was little protection for Chinese industry. A weak and usually divided government was able to do little to assist native Chinese industry, though later the Nationalist government resumed considerable control over external trade relations. Western commercial interests were greedy and arrogant, but in the main had no political ambition. They were there for what they could make. Japanese commercial interests, however, saw themselves as the advance guard of an eventual total political and economic take-over of the whole country.

Sun, a sincere patriot, considered that he lacked the power and prestige to be the first president of the new republic and proposed instead the well-known strongman Yuan Shikai, known for his overt republican sympathies. Yuan, veteran general and courtier, former confidant of the Empress Dowager, commander of the new, well-equipped Beiyang army based in North China and enjoying foreign support, scheming and ambitious, was no true believer in democracy. He soon attempted to restore the monarchy with himself as emperor, an unpopular move which aroused widespread opposition. Rumour had it that he was in reality a toad with evil powers, and he was soon defeated by the new Republican army, dying of cancer soon after. Yuan had set up his headquarters in Beijing in 1916; Sun did the same for the South in Canton, and it was there that his Nationalist Party, or Guomindang, later set out to reunify a China whose politics were to remain militarized, with warlords vying for power and intermittent civil war. There was to be no united government in complete control of all China for a generation and by the early 1920s Sun's disappointment at the general lack of support and concern at growing Japanese aggression caused him to turn to the new Soviet Union for help. China had meanwhile entered World War I on the side of the allies largely to gain Western support for her attempts to resist Japanese encroachment, but was shabbily treated at the Versailles Treaty of 1919, resulting in the famous 4 May riots in Peking, a massive demonstration of Chinese public opinion, which succeeded in achieving restitution of Chinese rights over former German territory in Shandong, rather than for them to be handed over to Japan as proposed in the Treaty. This was part of the infamous Japanese 21 Demands presented earlier to the government in Peking, which would have reduced China to the status of Japanese colony. Sun was not a practical man and some of his aims were unrealistic, but he was tenacious. The Moscow Comintern sent a senior official, Mikhail Borodin, to help build a southern power base including the Whampoa military academy, commanded by the rising military star, originally Japanese trained Chiang Kai-shek, who from there planned to lead his army north to unify the country. Sun had meanwhile died in 1925 with his dreams unrealized; he is honoured to this day by all Chinese, and his rather doleful features are to be seen in portraits of the Chinese pantheon.

The Chinese Communist Party was founded in 1921 by a group of intellectuals in Shanghai. Inspired by the Bolshevik revolution and China's own 4 May movement, they accepted advice from Moscow that the quickest way to power was to ally themselves with the established party of reform and revolution, the Guomindang. Soon agitators had fomented a series of boycotts and protests throughout South China, chiefly based on class grievances and dislike of the heavy-handed foreign firms; there were riots and strikes including a lengthy seamen's and dockers' strike in 1922 in Canton and HongKong. In 1926 Chiang Kai-shek set off on his Northern Expedition and with Communist help had secured all South China by the following year. Meanwhile differences grew between the Left, which advocated redistribution of wealth and power, and the Right, which wanted to remake China but not by class war. In April 1927 Chiang struck at the Communists in Shanghai with a bloody purge. Thousands were killed, and many fled to the countryside, there to wage a civil war that lasted for over 20 years. The early

Communists were durable: Chairman Mao Zedong and his close comrades in arms, Zhou Enlai who later became prime minister and Zhu De the army commander, all became widely known, surviving wars and revolutions and coming to rule China. Meanwhile Chiang continued to march north, defeating or winning over a succession of warlords such as the diminutive Zhang Zuolin, dictator of Manchuria, Wu Peifu, Yan Xishan and the well-known Christian general, Feng Yuxiang, who reputedly baptized one of his army battalions with a hosepipe. By the summer of 1928 the Northern Expedition occupied Peking with mission accomplished. The capital of the Republic remained at Nanjing; but China was, on the face of it, more of less unified. The Communists, weakened but still active, were in continued rebellion against the government. The West, whose Shanghai business community had first viewed Chiang as a 'dangerous Red' due to his previous affiliation with the Communists, decided the new regime suited its book and was worth backing.

The Chinese civil war continued with a series of Nationalist Army military encirclements aimed at exterminating the Communist forces, particularly in the mountainous and remote areas of Jiangxi and Hunan provinces. Superb leadership by Mao and his comrades, skilful tactics and the enlistment of the aid and support of the local population enabled them to survive a planned campaign by vastly superior forces, advised and trained by a German military mission. It was about this time that Mao, the dominant person in the Communist party throughout, coined the memorable phrase that the people were the sea, and he and his men the fish that swam therein. By 1934 the pressure became so intense with the latest 'bandit suppression campaign' that the decision was taken to evacuate present bases and move to the other side of China. Some 60,000 troops and followers embarked upon the epic Long March which has passed into Chinese history; marched west, then north, ending up after a march of 20,000 li (say 6,000 miles) over a year later, having traversed nine provinces. Their route led over mountain and wasteland, high plateaux, turbulent rivers, often under attack either by pursuing government forces or local levies or, on occasion, hostile tribes. The new Communist base was at Yanan in Shaanxi province, and it was here that American journalist Edgar Snow met Mao and the Communist leadership and broke the story to the world in *Red Star over China*. Snow put Mao and his comrades on the map; in later years he was an honoured guest and would stand beside Mao at National day celebrations in Peking.

Despite civil war, disunity, the threat of outside aggression and massive economic problems, the general situation in early 1930s China was not all one of unrelieved gloom. Although there was some ruthless suppression of the opposition, thinkers and intellectuals were largely free to express themselves. What has been called 'the golden age' flourished at this time, with writers such as Ba Jin whose trilogy *Jia Chun Qiu* (Home Spring Autumn), a sort of Chinese Forsyte Saga, achieved great acclaim, the female novelist Ding Ling, the Manchu Lao She with his tales of ordinary Peking people, the poets Guo Moruo, Wen Yiduo, and the great Lu Xun whose essays and stories epitomized intellectual Chinese aspirations. A noted professor at Peking University, Hu Shi had meanwhile advocated that Chinese be written as it is spoken, calling for the abolition of the classical system whose archaic written language bore little or no relation to the spoken. This so-called literary revolution changed the way China wrote, and read, in the space of a few years. These same intellectuals, drawn from left and right, academia, the professions and a few bureaucrats, engaged in far-reaching debate, not just about the future of China. It became fashionable to read Western literature, and soon Chekhov, Dostoevsky, Shaw, Dickens, Proust and other major Western authors were readily available in translation. The press advanced too, and major newspapers carried international coverage from the agencies; some Chinese reporters travelled around, a few went abroad, and more foreigners came to China to write, to teach, to help, not just to make money.

From their base in northwest China the Communists negotiated with the Nationalists about forming a united front against what was increasingly obviously the common enemy, Japan. Chiang held his hand, hoping to suppress the Communists before taking on the Japanese. He was however pre-empted and his hand forced by a bizarre occurrence, the so-called Xian incident. Chiang had been invited to Xian, capital of Shaanxi province and not too far from the Communist base at Yanan, by Zhang Xueliang, successor to his father, Zhang Zuolin, warlord of Manchuria, and commanding a sizeable army. Zhang kidnapped Chiang and forced him to agree to form a united front against the common foe, thus bringing about a truce between Nationalists and Communists. This eventually led to the defeat of the former many years later, and the formation of the Peoples Republic. But no one, except perhaps Chiang himself, could foresee this as the Communist 8th Route Army, Zhang's North East Army and Chiang's Nationalist Army stood ready as a united front to fight Japan. Later Zhang was arrested and imprisoned for the rest of his life, though under increasingly easy conditions. He spent his old age in a villa with a golf course in Taiwan, and was finally released at the age of 90. Invited to return to live in his old home in China as a man who had changed the course of history, he declined, not wishing to be involved in political controversy any more.

Japan, after years of covert and overt aggression and provocation in Manchuria, and Shanghai, and Peking, launched an attack, the culmination of a process that had begun in 1895 when Korea first came under Japanese control. The Marco Polo Bridge, near Peking, was the scene of a clash which rapidly developed into an all-out Japanese offensive. The Sino–Japanese War, 1937–45, later of course subsumed into World War II, killed some 30 million or more Chinese, destroyed most of what industry China had, ravaged the countryside, and destroyed towns and cities. It also ruined whatever chance the Nationalist government ever had of successfully ruling and unifying China, and so ensured the eventual founding of the world's largest Communist state. Japanese troops raped and pillaged their way across China, conquering all North China in weeks. In occupied territories the smoking of opium and the cultivation of the opium poppy were encouraged to debase the Chinese; prisoners were sometimes beheaded, atrocities were commonplace. The infamous 'rape' of Nanjing killed 300,000 civilians in a few days. The Nationalist Army, ill-armed, often not too well led, fought bravely; the so-called 'ragged battalions' after months of retreat had one big victory over the Japanese but failed to follow it up. But in the main it was defeat and loss of territory; the capital had to be moved all the way west to Chongqing. In these early years there was little outside help for China.

Then, in 1941 came Pearl Harbour and China was now an ally in the Free World struggle against fascism and the Axis, thus one of the Big Five at the Cairo Conference, and on paper at least a great power. Massive aid, nearly all American, flowed into China and Chinese troops fought alongside the British in Burma. Yet morale in the upper reaches of the Nationalist government and army was often low; corruption mounted, and rackets flourished. It was said that when some new tanks arrived, Chiang, by now known as the Generalissimo, personally had to allocate them to units. Meanwhile, the Communists had waged determined and skilful war, largely behind Japanese lines, and in so doing increased their support among the people. The behaviour of the Red *janshi*/'warriors' was exemplary, that of government soldiers all too often was not. By VJ day in 1945 the Guomindang government and its army was exhausted, corrupt and inept. The Communists were in the reverse position; they occupied more territory than before and by now had about a million men under arms, though receiving minimal aid from the Soviet Union. The incipient civil war started up again; the Americans sent General Marshall to mediate a truce, but talks broke down, and fighting between Communist and Nationalist resumed in 1946.

The Nationalists held by far the most territory having largely reoccupied Japanese held areas, even in some cases ordering the defeated Japanese to stay put until they arrived. However, not only were the Government forces largely demoralized, but China was in the throes of an economic disaster. Supplies were scarce, people starved, communications had broken down, the country had been laid waste by eight years of war; the government had a virtually impossible task. There was also rampant inflation and the entire banking system was breaking down. There were ugly stories of army recruits being marched through the streets tied to each other by ropes in case they tried to run away, even of wounded soldiers being asked for money by stretcher bearers. The agony continued to 1948 with a massive battle in central China, resulting in total Communist victory and Nationalist rout; whole units sometimes surrendered and, after some retraining and indoctrination, joined the Communist side. Many Chinese prayed for an end to the suffering, not caring who won. Finally, defeated Nationalist troops retreated to Taiwan, where they had already bloodily suppressed a rising. In Peking, on 1 October 1949, Mao Zedong proclaimed the foundation of the People's Republic of China, saying in his high-pitched voice 'The Chinese people have stood up'. The world watched and waited. The United States continued to support its ally Chiang Kai-shek and his now defeated government and army on Taiwan; a long period of Sino–US hostility had begun and the US 7th Fleet patrolled the Taiwan Straits, rendering an immediate attack impossible. Most nations quickly recognized the new China whose policy was, as Mao so clearly put it, to 'lean to one side'; China was firmly in the pro-Soviet camp.

In the summer of 1950 Communist North Korean troops invaded the south in a straight take-over bid. The United Nations sent a force, principally American, which pushed the North Koreans back up to the Chinese border. China then entered the war with a large army of 'volunteers', beating back the UN force but incurring very heavy casualties through tactics such as '*renhai*/human sea' charges, i.e. massive frontal infantry assaults against greatly superior UN firepower. Eventually, in 1953, a truce was called on the 38th parallel, which remains the frontier between the two states of Korea. These were not peaceful times for China; in 1950 she invaded and conquered Tibet, always considered part of the Middle Kingdom, in 1953–4 she intervened with undeclared aid, including specialist troops, in the French Indo-China war, and in the late 1950s there were aerial dogfights in the

Taiwan Straits and artillery duels with Nationalist artillery positions on the island close to Xiamen, on the Fujian coast. The huge army also mopped up any residual resistance after victory, or Liberation as it was called in 1949, in some cases chasing remnants out of the country, for example into Burma. There was also tension on the border with India, and a small scale Chinese invasion in 1959–60. After the Sino–Soviet split there were incidents on the Russian border, and of course Chinese assistance to the Vietnamese during their war with the Americans. In all cases China was fulfilling the age-old policy of maintaining her security and territorial integrity by assuring that all the states on her borders were at best subservient, at worst neutral. China's vast volunteer army not only defended the borders and garrisoned the towns and countryside, it also engaged in reconstruction.

When China's leaders formulated a strategy for rebuilding the nation, they followed certain principles including: a command economy; abolition of private ownership; the unquestioned leadership of the Communist Party; collectivized agriculture; and a one-party state. There was also a strong appeal to nationalism; many Chinese who disliked the new regime were yet pleased and proud to see their country strong again and treated with respect abroad. Indeed, the world view on China changed rapidly; from an object of pity, even at times contempt, not to be taken too seriously, to something quite different. Many people were now slightly afraid of China, a sealed country, within whose borders no one knew what was going on, that did not really enter into dialogue but made statements. China, having got rid of the landlords and capitalists, usually by confiscation and a set of brutal purges, then introduced cooperative farming which all peasants had to join. Intensive reconstruction repaired the roads and rebuilt the towns, new industry was sited, often indiscriminately, as it was believed every district should, for example, be able to make its own bricks; so in every town there was a kiln and one would see a pile of coal dust at every railway siding, and a tall factory chimney nearby. A series of five-year plans set production targets in industry and agriculture. Tight fiscal control and the elimination of private banking rapidly reduced inflation. Education was basic and available to nearly all, children learned to read and write, simple arithmetic and history with a patriotic slant. Food was distributed to famine areas, public health improved, law and order prevailed. Things were rapidly getting better.

It has been argued that the Confucian concept, whereby the welfare of the community may override the importance of the individual, and that people may surrender some liberty for security, had a bearing on the widespread acceptance of the Communist system. There was also considerable coercion. A vast public security system ensured universal compliance, including a network of labour reform camps where inmates worked and underwent 'brainwashing' until they were adjudged reformed. Society in town and country was in time disciplined and organized with the Party in command; all in responsible positions were Party members. After Liberation, a massive inquisition took place and people were categorized, the majority who passed muster were left alone, those who could be viewed as class enemies through their views or background were purged. Following confession and self-criticism they would be sent to camps for reform, or in some cases prison. Any organized opposition to the regime was virtually impossible due to the effective system of surveillance and control; neighbour reported on neighbour, in extreme cases children reported on parents. Most Chinese compared the security and order the Communists brought to China with the misery, starvation and confusion of the previous 20 years. Unless a person acted individually and rejected the system, or had a reactionary or class enemy background, he or she was safe enough. In most areas the system was imposed on a local basis and thus varied in severity. Some intellectuals who left China at that time described life as acceptable, but narrow and boring.

In 1957 came the first example of Mao's idiosyncratic leadership, the 'Hundred Flowers Movement' when he invited everyone to come forward with their views, no matter what those might be. Many intellectuals who had kept silent over the years now spoke up; their response and widespread disagreement with Party policy shocked the leadership, who called an immediate halt. Some of the outspoken critics were then in serious trouble and were criticized for deviating from the correct party line. In 1958 the Chairman had a more ambitious plan, the 'Great Leap Forward', whereby China would eventually catch up with the industrial West. This was to be done through the people raising production in their towns and villages, through forced collectivization with the aim of rapid industrialization of a peasant society. Millions were mobilized to construct dams and other public works, and people were forced into communal living with men and women in separate barracks. So came about the famous backyard furnaces, and other impractical notions; officials falsified the production figures and did not dare tell the truth that these new home-grown industries and new measures were unworkable. But what really mattered was that agriculture suffered mightily; it had not long recovered and production was rising not only enough to feed everyone, but also to pay for industrialization. This new direction caused widespread starvation and people died in millions. It was a disaster cloaked from the outside world until the evidence became too apparent to be denied. You could see the pinched faces of half-starved peasants in Canton in 1961, and rumours spread from new arrivals coming into HongKong.

Such a blow necessitated a reappraisal by the leadership. At the Lushan Conference in 1959, Mao was allowed to retain his position as Chairman but shunted to one side. A practical triumvirate led by Liu Shaoqi ran the country on orthodox lines and progress resumed. Meanwhile, China and the Soviet Union reached an ideological disagreement, basically because the Chinese did not accept Soviet leadership of the world Communist movement and were suspicious of Moscow's talk of peaceful co-existence with the West. There was a major split and thousands of Russian technicians were immediately withdrawn. China then progressed uneventfully until 1965 when Mao, aided by top soldier and 'close comrade in arms' Lin Biao launched a quite remarkable comeback, reasserting his authority by declaring war on his Party. The method used was fiendishly ingenious, inviting the young people of China to smash the old, be it schools, or institutions, or relics, or people who were not true revolutionaries with a 'red sun in their hearts', thus destroying the system and asserting Mao's rule. By late 1966, the Great Proletarian Cultural Revolution was in full swing: it was of course neither proletarian nor cultural, nor a spontaneous revolution. But everywhere the youth were unleashed, mostly organized as Red Guards, marching, meeting, demanding, smashing, terrorizing ordinary people. China was in turmoil and no one knew what was going on, still less was anyone in complete control. Mao himself was the centre of hysterical adulation. There was violence that spilled over into HongKong; production was affected and it was later estimated that China's education system was set back by about ten years. Many suffered, including officials found wanting who were banished to the countryside to 'repair the earth', a Chinese slang term for digging the soil. At one stage the few traffic lights then in Peking were changed; red no longer meant stop but go, in accordance with the Chairman's red revolution. Those who equated red with stop were counter-revolutionaries.

It was only a long time later than the damaging effects of the Cultural Revolution – more or less over by 1972, officially ended in 1976 – were fully evaluated. The precise death toll is still not known; there were few executions as such, but many deaths caused by beating, starvation and hard labour under harsh conditions. There were also numerous suicides, victims harried and persecuted to the point of taking their own lives. The Red Guard movement was by no means a unified force, though its members largely shared the same destructive aims. There was factional in-fighting between rival groups, and it became hard to know who was who. The already overloaded transportation system was frequently monopolized by Red Guards on the move, with rallies of up to a million people gathered to praise Mao, the Great Helmsman. Fortunately for China, the People's Liberation Army was relatively unaffected and stood firm, and was in time used to control the Red Guards. In many parts of the country the army replaced the banished or disgraced cadres and officials who had fallen victim to the Revolution, and so filled a vaccuum. China did not collapse and the business of administration somehow carried on, albeit directed by an apparently rudderless leadership. When it was all over, some citizens were compensated, though the government still referred to the 'gains' of the Cultural Revolution almost until the beginning of the Open Door policy. During this appalling episode, foreign trade declined, production slumped and there were few coherent foreign relations. The young suffered worst of all, as education was disrupted and they learned nothing for years.

By 1972 things were calming down and returning to normal. The skilful and talented Zhou Enlai remained as Prime Minister during all this time and, to an extent, moderated Mao's madness. The close comrade, Lin Biao was then alleged to have plotted to kill Mao, he escaped by plane and crashed in Outer Mongolia, a story no one entirely believed. The American President, Richard Nixon, then made a historic visit to Peking and the ensuing 1972 Shanghai Communiqué ended 22 years of unremitting Sino–American hostility. Diplomatic relations were resumed and America recognized the People's Republic of China. Meanwhile, Mao's wife Jiang Qing, prime mover of what later was known as the Gang of Four, planned to usurp power after the death of the now ailing and elderly Chairman, whose final demise in 1976 was marked by signs and portents in the sky, as with the passing of an Emperor. The much liked and respected Zhou Enlai had meanwhile died a few months previously, followed by public outbursts of grief and mourning.

Mao's death was the last in a series of shocks this extraordinary man had dealt his country. The Chinese themselves after a time formed an official judgement on him, saying he was 'seven parts good, three parts bad'. Some thought the proportions should be the other way round. Meanwhile the Gang of Four failed in their attempt at a coup, and were arrested and publicly tried. The Chinese then saw the extraordinary spectacle of Madame Mao, wife and helpmeet of the Great Helmsman, herself on trial for crimes against the State. An interregnum followed with Hua Guofeng, Mao's anointed successor, as Chairman. All over China were posters showing the old Chairman, ensconced in an armchair, saying to an attentive Hua who leaned forward to listen, 'with you in charge I do not have to worry.' The decade drew to a close with the first public call for democratic government in many years. A well-known dissident, Wei Jingsheng stuck a poster on what was later called Democracy Wall in central Peking saying that now China was modernizing there was one more aspect that needed attention. This was the fifth modernization, democracy. Soon after the wall was closed and Wei was imprisoned.

What were publicized all over China as the blueprint for the future, the Four Modernizations, agriculture, industry, defence, science and technology were made the basic policy of the People's Republic first by Hua Guofeng, and then by Deng Xiaoping when he came to power in 1978. They were subsequently modified, but remain the central core of China's aims and are incorporated in the constitution, part of a reform programme that ran counter to all the aims of the Cultural Revolution. This same shift in emphasis was supported by the appointment of two like-minded reformers: Hu Yaobang as Party General Secretary and Zhao Ziyang as Prime Minister. Deng came to power popular with a public exhausted by the Cultural Revolution and Mao's eccentricities, and introduced a set of policies known as 'socialism with Chinese characteristics'. Agriculture was radically altered by the 'responsibility system' whereby peasants contracted land, gave a fixed amount of their production to the State, and kept the rest. Production soared. Industrial controls were relaxed and managers granted decision-making powers. Foreign trade was promoted, foreign investment welcomed, joint ventures with foreign firms permitted, and an increasing flow of information and ideas entered the country from abroad. Special Economic Zones with capitalist-style systems, sealed off from the rest of the country, appeared along the coast, in many cases in the same location as the old Treaty Ports. All these measures, part of the so-called Open Door, served to transform China's foreign trade which grew mightily; foreign investment also grew and within a few years it was estimated that about 20 per cent of Chinese business had a foreign partner, one way or another. Deng made several pithy and practical remarks. He encouraged his people by saying it was glorious to be rich, yet maintaining tight Party control over government, and also said that the colour of a cat did not matter as long as it caught mice; it is results that count. He set China on a path of growth and modernization by unleashing the pent-up energy and entrepreneurial skills of her people. Modern China had arrived.

Yet Deng's rule culminated in tragedy. Thousands of students massed in Tiananmen Square in central Peking in the summer of 1989 in peaceful protest against various problems including corruption, and calling for more democracy. Various attempts to get them to disperse failed, and finally heavily armed troops were sent in to clear the area; the ensuing bloodshed shocked the world. The old men who ran China thought they were dealing with a plot to overturn their rule; the young people believed that a truly modern China needed more freedom and self-determination. After the incident there was a news blackout all over the country, and the event is still not publicly mentioned. Ordinary citizens will talk about it and some will tell you how China lost face on that day, something they may say but cannot write. This is an aspect of new China that has lagged behind. Sooner or later pressure for a more democratic form of government will come from a people who have endured so much, and achieved so much.

The Chinese have suffered greatly throughout their long history, particularly in recent years. Things are now getting much better; the people are comparatively well off and secure, the country is stable. Short of unforeseen disaster the future looks good. It has taken a long time, but China has at last stood up.

8

Equality and Mutual Benefit: Talking Business, Both Ways

Chinese negotiating attitudes and styles tend to follow a certain pattern; they are not of course an exact science, and comment on the subject can only be opinion, based on experience or observation. The Western stance when talking business in China tends to be reactive; it is usually the Chinese who set the pace and the tone. It is obviously easier to deal in some fields than in others and another truism may be summarized as the more delicate the subject the harder the going. Yet it is not always so, and business negotiations in China can be full of surprises. However, as a general principle a fairly recent statement by a senior official in the State Education Commission usually holds good. Speaking privately, he said, 'For business it is the green light. For politics and education is it the red light', which summarizes official Chinese willingness to accept foreign business and technology but not necessarily foreign ideas. Indeed you could say it is easier to set up a factory than to publish a book, although this too, like everything else in China, is changing. Like most other undertakings in this country everything takes longer, and consequently costs more, than your original estimate. Indeed, there is one rule of thumb which almost invariably holds good. As pointed out earlier, any estimate of the time and commitment involved should be doubled. This applies both to the newcomer businessman, or the '*lao pengyou*/old friend', veteran of many visits. Some things have not changed at all.

The practical and tangible aspects of business negotiations in any form, be it trade, investment, technology transfer, taxation, training and so forth are already copiously documented. There are various publications containing facts and data over an enormous range of subjects, sometimes with articles on how to approach the China market, and what to do, or not do, when you get there. Advisers, experts, consultants, all of varying calibre are available. There are numerous seminars, conferences, studies etc. held outside China, nearly all organized and attended principally by Westerners. It is received knowledge that the China business scene is complex and difficult to understand and the market hard to tackle, that China today constitutes a profit seeking market economy without some of the usual market restraints, plus the remnants of a command economy, and one where rules and regulations are sometimes indeterminate and often determined by precedent. Westerners mostly approach the challenge with some modesty, conscious of their ignorance, anxious to learn, some even obsequiously so. The Chinese, although often painstaking in their preparations frequently have an imperfect or superficial knowledge of the West, but do not always realize this. If any advice may be offered at this juncture it is that no one should lightly embark upon business negotiations in China. It can be a daunting, drawn-out, time-consuming and expensive process albeit with goodwill on both sides and a general desire for negotiations to succeed. The slogan '*pingdeng huli*/equality and mutual benefit' still holds good.

It is generally accepted how certain Chinese views on foreigners came about, the factors that shaped these attitudes and their resultant negotiating styles. There were the Western reactions to all this and the behaviour patterns arising from the interaction of the two sides. Actual negotiations may be generally described as follows: two sides separated by a table and a gulf of cultural half-understanding, with the cut and thrust of discussion, the banal platitudes and the stately minuet of obligatory polite small talk. Throughout there is both suspicion, and goodwill, all gravely recorded as benchmarks of progress made, from memorandum of understanding to contract. The whole is compounded by differing perceptions from each side; for example, the Westerners often reading more into a Chinese statement or action than is warranted, or the Chinese perhaps attributing a Chinese-type motivation to Western actions, for example preserving face when admitting a mistake. The differences can be profound. But both sides are usually disposed to learn from each other, to make concessions if needed to bring matters to a successful conclusion. Until fairly recently there was sometimes a political element in the Chinese attitude which was consequently affected by non-commercial reasons.

At the time of the first contacts with the West, any foreign trade was tightly controlled on Chinese terms and considered by the Chinese to be granting a boon to barbarians; the West admired the Empire from afar. Then this changed to cynicism, and then contempt for a weak and moribund empire whose efforts to keep the barbarian out failed, and a Chinese negotiating stance that could not admit of equal relations with outsiders gave way to a wily and adroit skill at dealing when holding a bad hand of cards; prevaricating, delaying, obfuscating. Only a comparatively small number of Western firms entered into commercial negotiations; there was little direct business, and most dealing was handled by compradores. This term, in the eighteenth century, meant something quite different from the modern version, who is basically a shop owner who provides household provisions from stock on monthly credit; compradores (the term is originally Portuguese) bought entirely on their own account and sold on to foreign buyers: tea, silk, native produce. Again, entirely at their own risk, they sold to and collected money from Chinese buyers, including rapacious officials, supplied and victualled ships, business houses, and even armies.

Not only were Chinese forbidden to teach Chinese to foreigners who, with a very few exceptions, had no wish to learn it anyway, but it was also not done even to eat Chinese food among the Western communities on the China coast. There was virtually no social intercourse between the two sides at all, and mutual ignorance and misunderstanding was profound. A very small number of Chinese spoke a mostly limited English. The *lingua franca* in the ports was pidgin English; with a vocabulary of only a few hundred words it was the chief medium of communication between the races and in no way sufficient to express any depth of thinking. There was none of the cultural interest and mutual admiration that existed in Kipling's India between conquering sahib and defeated tribesman. Far from it; Chinese regarded Westerners generally as something remote and bizarre, potentially dangerous, to be avoided as much as possible. This general state of affairs changed somewhat over the years, but in the main a huge gulf remained. Even as late as 1946, after decades of civil war and invasion, upheaval and catastrophe, there were some Western businessmen in Shanghai who thought somehow that the *status quo* and the good old days of their commercial superiority could continue indefinitely.

After 1949, the Communists imposed a rigorous and effective system, which consisted of first one, then eight, Foreign Trade Corporations headquartered in Peking with branches in most major cities. These FTCs, as they came to be called, carried out all China's buying and selling, according to strict cash limits imposed by the Bank of China, which had complete control over all China's foreign currency dealings. Promotion was handled by the CCPIT, the China Council for the Promotion of International Trade. Similar bodies handled insurance, shipping and land transport. Only technology and capital goods to build the nation were imported, nothing else. Credit was never asked for (although this was got round on occasion by the euphemism of deferred payment), and terms were cash by irrevocable letter of credit; foreign letters of credit had to be reconfirmed by the Bank of China. There was no foreign investment in any form and no resident foreign business, save a few unfortunate managers who remained under virtual house arrest, in some cases for years, pending settlement of huge claims made by the authorities for alleged underpayment of staff dating back to the 1920s. One particular example was a Belgian whose government did nothing as he languished in Shanghai for years. It was calculated that if every Belgian citizen contributed a dollar or so he could be freed. The very occasional Belgian visitor would call on him with gifts from home. He remained in custody.

Equally there was virtually no contact between Western buyer and Chinese producer, or Western manufacturer and Chinese end-user, and everything went through the FTCs. On rare occasions, if for example the Chinese end-users could not understand how to operate machinery that had been bought, an engineer would be sent, in one or two possibly apocryphal cases, to switch the thing on. Meanwhile, the old guard of foreign business had withdrawn; after an interval some came back and a new type, many but not all with left-wing sympathies, operating from specialist trading houses in London and some European capitals, now played the game according to new rules. There was no inside track, no favours, no kickback, no corruption, no *houmen* or back door. Your credentials were your products and prices, your good faith, your reliability and your friendship. Doing business with China in the early years after 1949 was also a political act. It meant showing where your sympathies lay, although Chinese purchasing decisions were pragmatic unless of course the goods came from enemies such as the United States. This state of affairs lasted throughout the 1950s and the turmoil of the 1960s, then eased and enlarged in the 1970s, but in essence the same command structure governed all China's foreign trade relations for 30 years.

Attitudes towards China, and doing business with her, altered dramatically after 1949. No one quite knew what was going on and people were apprehensive. Westerners going to China on business were at great pains not to offend their hosts in any way, agreeing with their political statements, toughening up only when it came to the actual nuts and bolts of the deal. Tales of such sycophantic behaviour abound. A large London firm instructed its staff always to refer to Taiwan as 'your occupied territory'; the managing director of another prefaced every meeting with quotations from the little red book of Mao's sayings until the Chinese themselves quietly told him this was no longer necessary; a group of businessmen at a song and dance show in Tianjin vigorously applauded a stage mime of the shooting down of an American plane over Hanoi. For their part the Chinese kept you on your toes; a letter mistakenly addressed to the Republic of China, the defeated Nationalist regime, could be returned as 'not known here', or, if there was a delivery it would occur very late in the evening, with the recipient roused from his bed to hear a 40-minute harangue from a couple of indignant cadres. The Western businessmen of those days, with a few exceptions, accepted all this, and the tight system, and worked accordingly, knowing that an order could come two years after a presentation. These New China Hands, like their predecessors, knew little of Chinese culture, history and language; bending always with the wind, they agreed with Chinese propaganda. It was the business that mattered, that was their main aim. On the other side, the Chinese who dealt with the Westerners, the officials and the managers of the FTCs, were a small band of skilled, shrewd negotiators, honest, imbued with a strong sense of duty, ruthlessly pursuing the best deal possible for China. All dealings between two sides were formal, arrangements were cumbersome, delays considerable. But the system worked. And despite the vast cultural differences and distant personal relationships between the parties, there was sometimes just a hint of the camaraderie that exists among practitioners of a difficult art. This never went further than friendly conversation; any gifts were modest and to the organization rather than to the individual.

Some things were differently arranged then. One example, which probably attracted more attention, and entailed more effort, was travel to China on business. The only way to get to China was to be invited by an authorized body with whom you were doing business. The letter of invitation could take weeks to arrive, and every now and then a polite cabled reminder would be sent. On average the outward correspondence file with China in most firms was about ten times thicker than the inward. There were anxious phone calls to the embassy's consular section to ask if the letter of invitation was in; it was well to inquire under first name as well as surname as Chinese name order was often used. The next step was to fill in a lengthy visa application form which, among other, inquired about your religion and political party. Then came awaiting the visa itself, with departure date fast approaching and more anxious phone calls and visits. It was unwise to tell the visa clerk your actual departure date as the visa would only be issued the day before, the thinking being you would not need it before then. So finally you travelled into China by rail from HongKong, there being no other way save via Moscow, on foot carrying your bag over the bridge at Lowu, to undergo a lengthy but courteous immigration and customs inspection, followed by an excellent lunch, all part of the ticket. Revolutionary background music helped to while away the time; often this was folk music on native instruments, occasionally stentorian choruses singing marching tunes. Then you took another slow train up to Canton, arriving a few minutes too late for an onward connection to Peking.

Wherever your final destination, your host corporation would meet you, accompany you to your hotel, where another administrative ritual took place as you checked in. You could find a stranger's luggage already dumped on the other bed in your room; the Chinese did not let rooms as such, they let bed spaces and it took a long time for this to change. There were often emotional scenes in hotel lobbies as guests explained their predicament to impassive staff. Then came money-changing at the Bank of China counter, again necessitating form filling with full details. You lost your duplicate at your peril as it had to be presented on leaving the country as proof of foreign currency spent. This would usually be handled by a girl with long pigtails and grey cotton sleeve protectors who clicked away at an abacus, and slowly, helped by a colleague, flicked out a bundle of notes. Your passport was then impounded by your hosts, to be handed over to the Public Security Bureau who would return it just before your departure with the necessary exit permit. Not only did you need permission to go into China, but to get out of it too and this worried some people. Any internal travel, usually by rail, necessitated checking in at the Foreigners Check Point both at departure and destination. Whatever transaction you entered into, from paying a bill to using a taxi, your particulars were carefully logged: name, room number, unit. Payment was invariably slow as change always had to be given, down to the very last *fen*.

Western business visits to China any time between the early 1950s and the 1980s followed a pattern, much of which remains to varying degrees. As an example, two Western businessmen, a sales director and technical director have come to process further negotiations for the sale of plant and accessories to a Chinese factory. Having been to China before, they have come ready-armed with instant coffee, laxative, elastoplast, writing pads, carbon paper, TCP, Optrex and 60 watt lightbulbs, both screw-in and bayonet socket, 110 volts and 240 volts to supplement the invariably dim lighting in their rooms. They have dealt with the provincial foreign trade organization and indirectly through them the local industrial end-user. The groundwork for the deal has already been covered, a memorandum of understanding has been drawn up and both sides are prepared to go through it, point by point, to form the basis of a subsequent formal contract. It is 9.00 am and two men are sitting in the larger of their two bedrooms awaiting their hosts who arrive exactly on time with handshakes all round and enquiries as to their well being. The senior Chinese is deputy general manager of the corporation. He is accompanied by a manager, an assistant manager, an interpreter and an assistant. There may be another party present who throughout says absolutely nothing and whose function is indeterminate.

Before getting down to business there is a ten-minute exchange of polite and platitudinous small talk, including observations as to the value of friendship, the benefits of cooperating with old friends, mutual understanding and mutual benefit. The hosts also evince a remarkable interest in climatic conditions abroad, including a desire to know the temperature when their guests left home and the difference, up or down, when they arrived in China. If the visitors are English there may also be the obligatory remark about London fog. Polite surprise, tinged with disbelief, greets the remark that there is no more London fog. The visitors then may ask after someone they met last time and may be told the person is in south China, or north China, that is all. There is now usually a pause and the assistant, usually a girl, chips in with questions regarding the visitors' stay and itinerary, need for tickets, bookings and so forth. She also announces the programme for the next few days: dinner that night given by the general manager, an outing on Sunday, a factory visit, perhaps a theatre visit. She then gathers up her notepad, puts it in the inevitable CAAC China Airline bag and takes her leave.

The two parties are arranged on chairs around the room. One or two are borrowed from next door. Inevitably, room service now arrives to sweep out the room and are asked to come back later on which they do with an ill grace. Someone will then come to deliver the laundry. This has to be paid for in cash and the tiny sum involved almost always involves change which is never to hand. Then there follows a brief charade as to who will sit in the more comfortable chairs. The senior Chinese and the senior visitor sit side by side with an occasional table between them and the interpreter half opposite, half turning each time they talk to each other, which becomes uncomfortable after a while and often results in a crick in the neck. Tea is served in glasses from a thermos flask, the air is blue with cigarette smoke, jackets are divested. The attached bathroom is in regular use; as in all Chinese hotels, new or old, the plumbing is usually faulty and the constant trickle of water flowing into the cistern forms a background to the conversation. At 12.00 noon the Chinese leave for lunch, probably in another part of the hotel, followed by a sleep, to resume at 2.00 pm. The two Westerners likewise lunch together and compare notes. At 5.00 pm that afternoon talks end with handshakes all round once again. This is the daily pattern.

The assistant who made the arrangements then collects the visitors from their rooms at 6.00 pm and escorts them to another part of the hotel where there are private dining rooms, or downstairs to the lobby where after a brief but frantic search for the driver, a car takes them to a restaurant. The host, the general manager, his deputy who led the talks that day and the rest of the negotiating team, also possibly someone from the local government or end user, are waiting in an ante chamber. If it is in a traditional building they may sit in a room overlooking a courtyard, if as is increasingly common, a modern block there will be blinding neon light and glistening lavatorial wall tiles. Further introductions are made as necessary, the Chinese proffering visiting cards, often with two hands, as a mark of politeness; strictly speaking the correct thing is then to put the proffered card in the highest pocket possible, though that is now almost passé. Time was when Chinese officials had no cards, barely a name to boot, and told you absolutely nothing beyond the barest minimum about themselves or their job. In the early 1970s a joke visiting card was circulating among the small foreign community in Peking which bore the legend: 'The responsible official from the department concerned'. Everyone sits in large armchairs, or deep sofas with anti-macassars, or more frequently later, hard plastic settees, again always side by side, while tea is poured. There is the usual exchange of banal civilities.

The host then leads his guests to the table; there is a careful placement with principal guest on his right, deputy host opposite and second guest on his right and so on down the line. The guests are served with communal serving chopsticks placed in the middle of the table and eating begins. At about the third or fourth course the host proposes a toast to his guests and the success of the negotiations usually in *maotai*, an evil-smelling fire water, redolent of varnish, that is drunk on these occasions. Chinese style, the guests drink too; usually all remain seated, and later in the evening the senior guest proposes a return toast; it is a solecism to forget to do so. The conversation becomes more animated and the guests capacity for strong drink is noted and admired; a true toper is called '*hailiang*', i.e. he can swallow the sea. At about 8.00 pm the host announces that he feels sure the visitors feel tired (it has not been unknown in more recent years for all Chinese to leave punctually before 8.00 if there is to be a good programme on TV that night). Agreeing, they take their leave with yet more handshaking. There has been a general discussion though little actual business has been touched upon. Views have been exchanged and possibly a hint dropped or a suggestion made. Such occasions sometimes constitute the social highlight of the visit. Later, the hosts give a return dinner which they ask the Chinese to arrange for them. Often it is the same place, with similar menu.

The course of the negotiations is punctuated by one or more sight-seeing expeditions. Depending on numbers, this is in a minibus, known in Chinese slang as a bread wagon as it looks like a loaf. If in Peking, it will be to obvious venues such as the Great Wall, once uncrowded, now packed with tourists; there are also visits to museums, institutes, schools, factories as it is held that visits should be educational as well as recreational. Factory visits are preceded by a briefing in a reception room seated round a rectangular table; visitors hear a recital of facts followed by the usual request for comments or criticisms. Time was when they would be clapped by the workforce and rather sheepishly clap back. The calibre and seniority of the Chinese accompanying the visitors on these jaunts may depend on their status, or the level and state of the negotiations. A key factor is the interpreter and standards vary enormously; a bad interpreter can seriously hinder progress. Usually this is spotted early on by the Chinese side, some of whose members may know some English though they are loath to admit it. Very occasionally, the Westerners bring their own interpreter, or one of them, rarer still, speaks Chinese. Then progress is more rapid. So, after days or weeks, complex argument or simple dealing, an agreement of cooperation, or sale and purchase, is typed out in Chinese and English. It invariably contains a brief preamble, then lists all the clauses numerically. Usually there is little ambiguity; Chinese contracts are well drafted. There is usually a formal signing ceremony with photographs, with principals actually signing and all the other participants, hands behind the back, grouped behind staring straight at the camera.

Such was the Chinese attitude: polite, formal, conscious of protocol and procedure, with a set of rules you had to obey and could not possibly circumvent. There were no short cuts. You were in China because the authorities concerned considered your presence worthwhile and had accordingly invited you. Specialist advice and information from experts in a given field was of course welcome. Those Westerners who gave their views on other matters would be of course gravely listened to, and put right as necessary. We do not tell you how to run your country, do not tell us how to run ours. We accept, unquestioningly, the leadership of the Communist party for they are our hope for the future. We have eliminated the old evils of corruption, injustice, oppression, some caused in part at least by you. We are building a new society and reconstructing our country. You are welcome to help us. Our view is correct, there may be discussion, but acceptance of this axiom is mandatory. Of course there is freedom of speech in China but you must not speak in a reactionary fashion. There is no censorship either, but published material that is unfriendly is of course proscribed. We have democracy, *minzhu*, our people, '*min*', are the masters, '*zhu*', are they not? This new strident and confident approach did not necessarily supplant all earlier views, it overlay them. Much of the traditional thinking remained. Throughout, there was never any admission of failure. Face, national and departmental, was all important. Any mistakes were neatly rationalized. In short, the initiative had passed to the Chinese and the ball was in their court.

The Open Door reforms of 1978 when China admitted Western investment and freed her own economy had a dramatic effect on Chinese negotiating attitudes and styles. Certainly many aspects of doing business in China were affected to varying degrees. There began massive foreign investment, enough to play a major role in the economy which, apart from causing a great inflow of capital and know-how, resulted in comparatively sizeable Western communities living in Peking, Shanghai, Canton and, to a lesser degree, other major cities. These communities remain largely insulated from the mainstream of Chinese life, living together in designated areas, in flats, hotels or occasionally in houses, often at exorbitant rates. Again the age old Chinese accommodation of the foreigner can be detected. Nonetheless, Western and Chinese partners, executives and staff engaged in joint ventures meet regularly for discussion of business, there is frequent contact with various departments, and travel round China. The Special Economic Zones, the Development Areas, the regional autonomy that comes in fits and starts, the semi freeing of exchange control and banking, the stock exchange, the massive import of consumer goods, and the accompanying less attractive aspects of Western culture, together with the general loosening of restrictions overall, have combined to modify Chinese attitudes. Negotiations are sometimes more like everywhere else, and the trend will continue. But it is a slow and uneven process. China's recent accession to the World Trade organization will, of course, accelerate the pace of change as she will be competing globally on equal terms with less protection but more opportunity. She will also become increasingly involved in international issues such as protection of the environment, global warming and the atmosphere.

Business is still compartmentalized. Buying will not necessarily help selling as some foreigners fondly imagine. Nothing to do with us. A massive bureaucracy still squats overall, slow cumbersome, poor on lateral communications, decision by committee passed through a bottleneck of approval by the ubiquitous '*lingdao*/leadership' so often referred to. Each section or department is eager to defend its patch, and jealous of its privileges. The '*ganbu*/cadre', is alive and well. There is corruption in some high as well as low places, a relatively recent phenomenon, for in the days of the Chairman no such thing existed. There was privilege for senior Party members but it was rarely abused. Cynics said the absence of any corruption was because there were no opportunities. Some said it was fear. Confusingly, much of the so called private enterprise which has come about in recent years is not truly so in our sense. It is often provincial or municipal bodies, be they producers, manufacturers, transporters or administrators or whatever, who have been given the go ahead to seek markets, identify suppliers, fix prices, which they do together, in a sort of flexible combine originally rooted in a public enterprise. They thus do not undergo a large part of the enterprise formation process. The responsibility system, successful in agriculture, has had a mixed result in industry. The hardest thing on the modern Chinese scene is to find out exactly what someone does, exactly how his organization functions and how it interacts with others, and the demarcation of responsibility and authority. It is therefore very difficult for foreign investors, for example, to find the right partner for an enterprise, and include all the necessary ancillary organizations in the plan. Despite all the many new freedoms, there still remain many regulations and restrictions, some unpublished. The Chinese themselves are often not familiar with them either. It is hard to get a precise ruling. Some regulations are imposed in an arbitrary fashion. You never know your luck.

Certain basic Chinese characteristics governing attitudes and styles of negotiation present themselves. First, and overwhelmingly so, is the major cultural divide between differing codes of conduct, values and ethics. On the one hand there is the Confucian model of an ordered society where each has his place, refashioned by communism, sharpened by nationalism and now, under siege from materialism. On the other hand there is the broadly liberal enterprise ethic of the capitalist West, modulated by social responsibility, motivated by freedom, driven by profit. Westerners who talk socialism are regarded askance. Chinese are happier with Western capitalists who talk capitalism as they are easier to understand, and so, deal with. Confucian observance of hierarchy and seniority can still be observed any time in China. There is, far less than before, the original concept of the Middle Kingdom surrounded by barbarians, now principally manifested in Han racial superiority, to be seen sometimes in Han Chinese dealings with racial minorities. There are still popularly held misconceptions unwillingly abandoned, and often an unwillingness to try something new. As an example a senior official, stationed in London, does not read the local press at all. He gets all his information and comment on the Western scene from the week-old copy of the *People's Daily* he reads in his embassy.

Many Chinese often demonstrate a conviction of being right, thus past mistakes are explained away, 'we take from the past what is good, but leave what is bad.' The famous *guanxi,* which literally means connections, is as old as Chinese society itself the network of relationships, of obligations, of help due, the need for a *guanxi* to make an approach, the advantage of a *guanxi* in a particular organization when dealing with that organization. There is a general sameness of view and reaction as expressed to foreigners, plus an interest in the practical or that which impinges directly, rather than abstract concepts. So for example Chinese are usually more interested in the status of a Westerner with whom they are dealing, his position in his firm, his wealth, even how much he can drink than his opinion on a cultural matter which does not impinge. Most people you deal with appear reasonably content, though many younger officials dream of a lucrative career in the private sector. There is a widespread envy of Western technology and a passionate desire to catch up as fast as possible. This is now accompanied by an almost wholesale destruction of Chinese culture where native arts, in any form, have largely fallen into desuetude. Even the traditional Peking opera has been amended to suit tourist tastes. The scenes with duets and arias are cut, those with swordplay and juggling lengthened. Relics damaged during the Cultural Revolution have been repaired and in some cases grouped on the one site, even though separated by hundreds of years. This makes it more convenient for foreign friends to visit.

The enormous differences in language, expression and comprehension have also had a great effect on business negotiations of all sorts. Long ago, practically no one spoke the other's language at all with a very few exceptions: a handful of missionaries, the odd Chinese scholar who travelled abroad. Clear and coherent communication was virtually impossible, those involved relied on a mixture of guesswork and the totally inadequate pidgin English. Nowadays of course people try hard, particularly on the Chinese side. English has long supplanted Russian as the second language of the People's Republic and is taught in schools all over the country. Millions of young Chinese have a grasp of the language and will try and practise it where they can; this has indeed been the case for many years and an indication of the political barometer of the time was the frequency with which visiting foreigners were accosted in the street by students wishing to talk. There is nothing like a corresponding interest on the Western side, particularly among the business community, though there are more Western speakers than before. The standard of learning of each other's language remains variable, and interpreters frequently get it wrong, though the probably apocryphal story of the English trader at the Canton Fair who found he was getting nowhere each time he suggested the price be reduced and subequently found that when translated each time it was increased is no longer likely. One failing on the Chinese side is sometimes an unwillingness to admit a mistake, or ignorance, or a failure to understand, and this can occur on occasion with interpreters. An entire discussion can go completely adrift. Such difficulties are of course exacerbated by Westerners who mumble, have strong regional accents, use double negatives or convoluted speech construction. It can of course occur the other way too; an English group, one of whom spoke good Chinese, had as interlocutor a man speaking Mandarin but with a strong regional Hunan accent, which makes every 'h' into an 'f', and a cleft palate to boot. He could not understand why there was any difficulty.

The very nature of the Chinese language, that it is tonal, has no Western style syntax, is written in a series of ideograms, each one individual, makes for a massive conceptual gap. Language difficulties are a very real problem, not just what is said which can of course be wrongly translated, but the flavour and the protocol as well. Get something wrong and not only are you demonstrating your own ignorance, but lack of respect for your host. Apart from such general difficulties there are the specific problems that some words are virtually untranslatable, either way. Yet of course there is nothing, be it fact or idea, that cannot be expressed in Chinese and this ancient language has been readily adapted to modern phraseology. There are also the numerous subtleties or oblique terminology that when interpreted directly into a Western language give a slightly bizarre flavour. Thus it is fair to assume, particularly when making a request, that the Chinese answer of 'maybe' means 'no', that 'it is hard to say' when replying to a question as to how something was means 'it is terrible', and so forth. All this goes to show an added dimension of difficulty when Westerners talk business with Chinese. When checking contracts or other official and important documents, it is best to deal with the text paragraph by paragraph, rather than sentence by sentence. There is of course now an increasing foreign influence. Ask for something at the reception of any big hotel and you may well hear '*meiyou wenti*', which means 'no problem'. Also some Chinese who speak English will at times break into a jargon where many nouns and verbs in a sentence are in English, the link words Chinese. Some HongKong Cantonese speak tonal English.

From all this may be extrapolated certain fixed basic Chinese attitudes in business negotiations today. First comes secrecy, less than before when it was almost paranoid, but still there; partly this stems from anxiety over security and an unwillingness to admit defects or weakness which could lead to the advantage of any hostile party. More generally, there is the fear of losing face. As an example, Chinese officials would not specify buying requirements when planning Western industrial exhibitions as disclosure of needs could disclose weakness and deficiencies. They would only say they wished to see advanced technology; when pressed, they said they wished to see the newest advanced technology. Now of course there is far more commercial frankness, and Chinese buyers will even contemplate buying second hand. Yet still you are not told anything unnecessarily; this can even include items that have been published in the press. You will still find a door symbolically locked, a gate barred unnecessarily. Past misfortunes are first hidden, then are explained away; for many years just about everything was laid at the door of the Gang of Four. By the same token, saintly qualities are attributed to past heroes such as Zhou Enlai. Chinese secretiveness also stems from a general suspicion of Western business, its methods and motives and not without foundation. It takes time to build confidence. There is considerable cynicism and disinterested action is looked at askance. What is in it for them? Why should they bother? There is ruthlessness in negotiation, and self-righteousness. All this leads to the well known Chinese conduct of negotiations according to a set of rules which they consider correct and fair, and which rules they reserve to right to alter, sometimes retrospectively. This moving of the goalposts is also sometimes refined by negotiating the same contract with more than one party at the same time to see which one works out best.

Certain established commercial practices were flouted in the years after the Open Door, probably due to inexperience. Agents and middlemen were bypassed. Products manufactured in China as part of a buy back agreement were shipped direct, at a far lower price, to the original market, causing consternation. Conventional payment terms are not always observed; payment is sometimes demanded not within 30 days, but on the nail; later payment brings a surcharge. There is a moral high ground which is still occasionally invoked. If we have got it wrong, please be understanding. it is indeed your duty to help us, to make up for what you did to us before. Meanwhile everything possible may be extracted from the foreigner and indeed it has been said that a partner is often regarded as a resource, equally Chinese seem to believe their interlocutors make an enormous margin, loading their quotations by 20 per cent. We Westerners should anyway pay more because we have more capital and this justifies the often extortionate charges made for goods and services. China must be the only country in the world where not only are you very heavily charged for every minute of an overseas telephone call, but full tariff starts to apply after three rings whether you get through or not. On a more personal note, the Westerner is regarded with what may be described as cordial indifference. There is curiosity about his personal wealth, a rapid identification of the extent of his authority, big shot or 'small potato', and an assessment of his capacity for strong drink. In the main, Chinese at the negotiating table are not too exercised about what their opposite numbers are thinking, apart of course from the subject under discussion, where the concentration is intense. Apart from these practical considerations there is little intellectual curiosity. All these fundamental attitudes give rise to a distinctive style.

The Chinese style of negotiation is polite, courteous, grave, painstaking, thorough, indefatigable. There are no flamboyant gestures, very rarely any sign of annoyance and then restrained. They know how to press home an advantage. Equally they know how far a point may be pursued, when to let up, even, it has been known, going to the airport to persuade the other side not to leave. This subtle style also includes the provision of a ladder by which either party may descend if necessary; no one should ever be pushed into a corner from which there is no retreat. Smilingly they will on occasion make those oft recorded unreasonable demands; come back again next month, stay on over Christmas, send half a ton of samples at once by air, get this contract typed today as we cannot do it ourselves. Westerners who readily agree to this sort of thing gain no advantage and will soon be asked for more. A refusal does not offend and is often accepted with amusement. It is also fair game to suck the Westerner dry for information and requests for help; reference books, however arcane, instructions, ring up your embassy to enquire why their visas for a visit to your country have not yet been granted (usual answer: the application was only lodged yesterday). There is a meticulous thoroughness which will permit an entire day being spent hearing a presentation they have already decided to reject, just in case there is some new nugget not to be missed, a small advantage to be gained. You cannot pressurize them, and threats never work.

The actual negotiating process is unhurried. There are breaks while the Chinese team refers back to higher authority for guidance and delays if parallel organizations are consulted, as lateral communications are poor. Things go right up to the top, across, then right down again. There is no picking up the phone for an informal word with colleagues in another department next door, unless of course there is a *guanxi* to hand. As discussions progress and new aspects come to light, the Western side will very likely need information and guidance on who further should be consulted, or brought into the discussions, for example, customs, the local electricity supply organizations, the railways. The Chinese side will certainly provide both information and introductions, but only when asked. They will not necessarily volunteer it. Regulations, edicts from Peking are noted, quoted, and on occasion bent. So the permissible sum that may be invested without central approval may perhaps be doubled by having two identical projects, likewise for example the floorspace of a trade show. Taxation and fiscal regulations, customs dues and the like are not always properly understood by either side and there is considerable speculation to how they apply. Even the specialist accountants now established in major cities that advise Western firms on such matters have great difficulties in arriving at the exact situation. These organizations charge very high fees and it has been known for the final bill to be higher than the sum under review. All too often they have not got to the bottom of the matter either; many of the resident staff are from HongKong, knowing almost as little about China as do their Western directors.

Then the pattern of the negotiations begins to unfold with the first marker, the memorandum of understanding, which states, usually in general terms, the degree of agreement reached so far. Inevitably it has a preamble which describes how both sides met and held friendly discussions. It is valued by the Chinese as a benchmark, it is a useful record, and it is submitted to a higher authority as evidence of progress made. Next follows the Letter of Intent, a mark of further progress, more precise, more specific, implying a degree of commitment. Lastly comes the actual contract, born of days, weeks, months of negotiations, in the two languages. Both versions are always considered to have equal force, though the Chinese is deemed to be superior in case of any contradiction, which contradicts the standard preamble to all contracts which states that both languages are the same. Contracts are usually well drafted and reasonably precise and sometimes may be amended in the light of further developments. They can on occasion be altered informally, with the concurrence of both sides, to iron out a problem without necessarily going through any formal re-negotiation process and the necessary approval from higher authority all over again. It is instructive to watch how the deft deletion or inclusion of a character or two can achieve such an aim, though such subtle redrafting obviously cannot usually apply to the English.

There are numerous difficulties and frustrations. Chinese do not always see the need to answer correspondence promptly. Nowadays this may be because many offices switch off their electrical supply at the end of the day; or sometimes no need to reply at all is perceived. In one classic instance an urgent, indeed vital, consignment of goods for a major technical exhibition was the subject of repeated, increasingly frantic, requests for confirmation of safe receipt. Finally, when all concerned met, the official responsible pointed out that no reply meant the goods had arrived. So they would only get in touch had they not arrived, surely this was obvious? Administrative arrangements can get muddled, changes in address and phone are not always notified, paragraphs are wrongly numbered; drivers lose their way; arrangements for hotels, accommodation etc. have to be checked, and checked again. It is still a golden rule when travelling in China that when you arrive anywhere, the first thing that you must do is find out about leaving. Also, of course, set aside half a day for making the necessary arrangements and on the day itself check in at airport or railway station at least two hours early. There may be an extra security procedure, or change in schedule. Your Chinese hosts, if involved will see you do all this anyway; indeed they will worry greatly until you are on your way and off their hands.

In general, the Western side reacts rather than initiates, with the obvious exception of submitting proposals. It also has to provide fullest technical details and supply any information requested, a vital prerequisite to any business. As noted already, it was usual for Westerners in the days of Mao to go to China in a supplicatory role, bending over backwards to be agreeable, enthusiastically agreeing with their hosts' views on everything. There is no way of knowing how much business this brought them. The Chinese negotiators gravely accepted all this as their due and, more than now, continued to occupy the moral high ground. Nowadays, much has changed. But many Westerners still eat sea slugs for fear of offending their hosts, or put up with delays and inefficiencies without a murmur, or acquiesce in being blatantly overcharged. Chinese abroad are different; many do not like Western food and say so, and make it clear if they are not happy with the arrangements. Often the Chinese mission pays its airfares and not much else; the rest is up to the Western host, even on occasion pocket money. Western visitors travelling round China not only pay their way entirely, but on occasion for the Chinese hosts accompanying them, and no-one argues about this. This general Chinese advantage continues throughout negotiations, with Westerners worrying what the Chinese are thinking, and spending many hours in speculation. That they have little else to do may have some bearing on this. Some try to analyse Chinese motivation and action into Western patterns. One or two organizations have gone so far as to analyse the Chinese decision-making process by business school methods, with ludicrous diagrams and flow sheets. Western attempts at humour, often made against all advice, invariably flop as they are usually very hard to translate and if understood by the Chinese are probably not funny anyway.

There are some conclusions to be drawn. Chinese negotiating attitudes and styles are altering but at an uneven pace. As China modernizes and the market develops, so will the business process become easier inasmuch as it will become more like that obtaining everywhere else. Yet differences and difficulties will remain and China is not going to become an easy market. Increasing Western familiarity with conditions may lead to a confidence which at times proves to be a false friend. It is most important to remember that, whatever the situation, there is usually goodwill. Chinese are not out to make things difficult *per se*. It is just that they often see things differently, and so work in a different way. This state of affairs will continue for a long time; some aspects for ever. Furthermore, there are really no short cuts and, for Westerners, no inside track. You must still play the game according to the rules.

Entering into the Chinese business negotiation process is a definite, long-term commitment, demanding, time consuming and expensive. Western businessmen should be clear as to their priorities, as it is no good including China as a side-show. You must send your best people and make a major effort. Small firms should carefully appraise their resources, not only financial, but in able and competent directors and managers who can cope with situations, make decisions and exercise judgement.

9

Within the Four Seas: Compatriots at Home and Abroad

Over fifty million Chinese live outside the mainland of China. Nearly half inhabit the island of Taiwan, separated by the Formosa Straits from the province of Fujian. This was the seat of the opposition Nationalist regime that fled the mainland following defeat at the hands of the Communists in 1949, still calling itself the Republic of China and claiming to be the legitimate government of all China. It is now under a democratically elected government and remains opposed to eventual reunification with the mainland. A further six million live in the formerly British administered colony of HongKong, since 1997 a special administrative region of China. These people, and the inhabitants of the former Portuguese administered Macao, are known as '*tung bao*/same womb compatriots'. Although HongKong and Macao are now reunified with China, lifestyle, management and general business practices remain very largely as before. The citizens of these two administrative regions enjoy a different status to their compatriots on the mainland.

The remainder are known as '*huaqiao*/Chinese living abroad', usually referred to as Overseas Chinese and are mostly settled in '*Nanyang*/Southern Ocean' or South East Asia. In some instances they form the majority or large part of the population as in Singapore and Malaysia, or a small but commercially powerful minority as in Indonesia. Throughout the region they have come to control most of the economy though do not play a prominent role politically. There are also small pockets of Overseas Chinese scattered throughout the rest of the world; mainly in Japan, on the west coast of the United States, in Canada, Australia and Oceania. Despite their widely differing backgrounds, economic and social conditions, language, customs, even physical characteristics, all are Chinese and all share qualities of what has been described by a distinguished scholar as Chineseness.

Most of them look to their '*zuguo*/ancestral country' in varying degree. For reasons of pride of race, family ties and self-interest they wish to see a strong and prosperous China. Thus there is considerable inward investment; it is estimated for example that no less than 80 per cent of the compensation trading deals that have been signed in China since 1978 have been made by the compatriots of HongKong alone. Relatives in the seaboard provinces of Guangdong and Fujian, ancestral home of most Overseas Chinese, still sometimes receive remittances from kinsmen they have not seen for a generation. HongKong Chinese also regularly remit large sums over the border to families in Guangdong and beyond. There is a large and steady stream of visitors to China where the majority of tourists are themselves Chinese, looking up family ties, bearing gifts, visiting the graves of ancestors, investigating business possibilities, touring a country most of them have never seen, whose national language they often speak indifferently or not at all, whose written language they sometimes can no longer read or write. The Overseas Chinese and the HongKong–Macao compatriots regard China with a mixture of respect, curiosity and affection, at times exasperation, and, on occasion, apprehension. The first-time visitor from San Francisco will have American ideas on order and hygiene, the HongKong Chinese may expect rapid fire response and high efficiency, the Singaporean may look for Western-style comfort and technology. Sometimes they will be disappointed, and all will also find that despite the ethnic similarity of background, their fellow Chinese in China are unlike the people back home.

There is evidence that the first Chinese settlements in Nanyang occurred in the distant past, during the Han dynasty about 2,000 years ago. Later, voyages of exploration during the fifteenth century at the time of the Ming dynasty started a series of small Chinese colonies, principally at Malacca on the Malayan coast, in South Sumatra and in Java. These enclaves grew and prospered, fostered by energetic, hard-working people who maintained a small but steady trade, carried in large ocean-going junks, with their home provinces of Guangdong and Fujian. These were the very original founders of the *China Peranakan*, or Chinese indigenous to the region, later also known in Malaya and Singapore as Straits Chinese. In the mid-nineteenth century there was a further influx of Hokien (Fujian) immigrants to Malaya many of whom prospected for tin; they were followed by a wave of Hakka (Kejia), fleeing from the aftermath of the Taiping rebellion. Then, in the late nineteenth century, when rubber began to be grown in the region and the local people were largely unwilling to work on the estates, there arose a pressing need for labour. Contractors toured the coastal villages of south east China and further inland, signing up coolies by the thousand, who were indentured and shipped south, packed on the decks and in the holds of trampships to work out their contracts. This great influx of Chinese labour permanently altered the economy of the region, many never returned home, and of those who stayed some prospered, becoming towkays or merchants, grouping together in the towns and settlements, often specializing in certain trades, usually supporting each other via clansmen or local associations. Thus grew complete Chinese quarters in major cities such as Batavia, now Jakarta, Surabaya and Kuala Lumpur. There were also Chinese community leaders responsible for law and order to the authorities; in British territories known as the Kapitan China, and as time went by, Chinese lawyers, doctors, accountants, clerks and administrators. The chief Chinese activity was business and manufacture, and some established great commercial empires that continue to this day.

HongKong was an insignificant settlement of a few fishing villages when the British took it in 1841; its economy grew with its importance as a port and commercial centre on the China coast. Macao, originally occupied by the Portuguese with Chinese consent as a trading post, remained a quiet backwater. Taiwan, whose original inhabitants were aboriginal tribespeople, was first colonized by Chinese during the Han dynasty as Chinese civilization spread south and east across the country, becoming later at times a haven for pirates and smugglers, the lair of bandits such as Koxhinga, who terrorized the island in the sixteenth century, or a bolt hole for deposed dynasties and defeated generals. Chinese reached the west coast of the United States by the 1850s to work as labourers on the new railroads or at the goldfields, also Australia where they went to work in the sugar cane fields of Queensland. They reached Liverpool, London and other European ports as sailors off ships, some to settle and set up the traditional laundries and restaurants, usually grouped in a small Chinese ghetto invariably known as Chinatown. Large numbers settled on the west coast of the USA and Canada, some to work on the railroads, others attracted by the goldfields of California and British Columbia. They reached Oceania as traders in the South Sea Islands, also South America and the Caribbean. Later there were a great number, nearly 200,000, of labourers transported to France during World War I to dig fortifications and build roads, China's contribution to the allied war effort, a few of whom remained behind. Those labourers who were killed in the fighting or died in the postwar influenza epidemic are buried in a military cemetery on the banks of the Somme, not far from Abbeville.

There was virtually no restriction on immigration into the colonial territories of South East Asia where the cheap labour was welcome. Taiwan was incorporated as a full province of China in the late nineteenth century and attracted settlers from the mainland without hindrance. Cantonese were permitted relatively free access to HongKong throughout British rule. Belatedly the Manchu government took note of what was happening and made some rather feeble representations on behalf of their people abroad. It was only with the collapse of the empire in 1912 that Chinese governments began to take any serious interest in Overseas Chinese. Attempts were made to exert some political and cultural influence and encourage loyalty to China. Thus by the 1930s every Overseas Chinese centre had its branch of the Guomindang or Nationalist party, and later, though often proscribed by the governments of the day, the Communist party. There was a traditional official view, vaguely observed, that all Chinese no matter who, no matter where, belonged to China and nowhere else; this existed until the early 1960s when, in a notable statement, Prime Minister Zhou Enlai encouraged Overseas Chinese to be loyal to the countries of their adoption, yet retain links with the motherland.

During World War II, most of the resistance to the Japanese in South East Asia was by Chinese who suffered greatly in consequence. China had of course already been at war with Japan since 1937 and by the time of the Japanese occupation of South East Asia in 1942, the War of Resistance had already been going for five years. There was notable resistance to the Japanese by Malayan Chinese guerrillas who, with a few British officers, went deep in to the jungle and stayed there, emerging to attack Japanese transport and military installations. After the war a series of Marxist-inspired rebellions, most of whose members were Chinese, and whose leaders looked to Mao Zedong and the Chinese Communist party as their guide, largely poisoned relations between China and the region. Of particular note was what was termed the Malayan Emergency, a long (1948–60) war of attrition between the Malayan Peoples Liberation Army, some of them members of the wartime resistance and the British-led security forces. Despite rumours to the contrary, the insurgents received encouragement from China, but little else; no arms were supplied if only because it was too difficult. This was also the case with the Hukbalahap Communist insurgents in the Philippines. There was of course Chinese support for the Vietnamese Communists during both the Vietnam wars which contributed materially to their final victory; at the decisive French defeat at Dien Bien Phu, Chinese gunners and engineers took part in the battle. There was also continued supply of arms and material via the Ho Chi Minh trail from China into North Vietnam. Vietnamese treatment of resident Chinese and territorial disputes in the South China Sea later soured relations, and there was a border incursion by China in 1979; the situation has since improved.

After 1949 there was a brief period of uncertainty over HongKong. It was accepted that it was British controlled, that large numbers of refugees had crowded in to the colony, and it was a place with which China had no formal political relationship. In practice, relations remained quite good except during the onset of the Cultural Revolution when local Maoists instigated a series of riots and bomb outrages and a Chinese attack over the border seemed possible. Meanwhile over the years, as HongKong ceased to rely on a dying entrepot trade and became a vital centre of manufacture and finance, so it came to play an increasingly significant role in Chinese development; nearly 40 per cent of China's badly needed foreign exchange was earned through the colony. HongKong also became the chief window on China, the neutral ground where discreet, unofficial contact between communist and capitalist could take place without anyone the wiser, where sworn enemies could talk without embarrassment, where all things were possible. The only way into China was via HongKong, save via Moscow, and there you could find out more about what was going on in China than from anywhere else. Taiwan was also a totally different matter; the base of a defeated government that, sheltering behind an American blockade, was able to state publicly its intention of resuming the government of China. All economic and commercial relations were frozen, though in time indirect trade began to grow. Now, like practically everything else inside and outside China, this situation is altering.

Apart from sending money home, building commercial empires and diligently developing the agriculture and industry of South East Asia, certain Chinese abroad had political influence on affairs in China in the early twentieth century. Thus many of the members of the Tongmenghui, forerunners of the Guomindang which overthrew the Manchu dynasty, met and planned in Japan, as did some of the would-be constitutional reformers in the late nineteenth century. Dr Sun Yat-Sen, father of the Republic, left his native Guangdong province as a young man and lived for years in HongKong practising medicine. He was among Overseas Chinese in Canada when the news arrived of the famous Double Tenth, leading to the collapse of the Manchu empire, and hurried home. Dr Lim Boon Keng, an active early revolutionary who left behind an evocative account of the proclamation of the

Republic on January 1912, with guns booming and flags flying, was a Singaporean. Much of the money that financed the early revolutionaries was Overseas Chinese and it was often they who published the political tracts and even on occasion arranged the supply of arms; they have their place in modern Chinese history. All Chinese outside China are now highly regarded by the Peoples' Government, which recognizes the role they can play in modernization. There is a large and active Department for Overseas Chinese Affairs, with branches in some provinces, and a similar body for HongKong and Macao affairs. There is no separate body dealing with Taiwan affairs as such; it is regarded on the same basis as the other provinces of China.

A substantial minority of China's external trade lies with the countries of South East Asia, and this is largely in Overseas Chinese hands. Business has surged ahead in recent years despite setbacks, largely as a result of the Open Door Policy, aided by the region's own phenomenal growth. The balance of trade is heavily in favour of China; with substantial increases in exports; the reverse flow includes traditional Nanyang produce such as rubber, copra, palm oil, pepper and spices. The most dramatic increase has been with the most Chinese of these countries, Singapore, where two-way trade increased sevenfold in the decade after the Open Door Policy was announced and where commercial interests strive to provide an alternative to HongKong as a springboard for business with China. Throughout the region there exists a network of banks and trading houses, some wholly, some partly owned by China together with Overseas Chinese interests, doing business in Nanyang. There is a steady stream of visits and missions to China and the region is also supplying some of the managerial expertise that China needs so badly. Likewise, a procession of technical study groups and delegations from the People's Republic visits South East Asia, and there is increasing Chinese participation in local industrial and technical exhibitions. Mandarin has become more widespread and is understood and spoken throughout the region. A good proportion of Overseas Chinese can read Chinese and there is a flourishing press, apart from Indonesia, where it is proscribed.

Actual Chinese political relations with the various countries obviously have a bearing on the volume of business. Singapore, with a population nearly four-fifths Chinese, with Mandarin as an official language, has strong and increasing ties. Malaysia, with a 40 per cent Chinese population, now has diplomatic relations with China after years of estrangement. Indonesia, where a 3 per cent Chinese minority controls 60 per cent of the retail trade but possesses no political influence at all, and is on occasion persecuted, has had only tenuous relations. Formal relations were only re-established in 1990, a legacy of the allegedly Communist-inspired attempted coup of 1965. There is a limited amount of direct trade with China; though most trade remains indirect, largely via Singapore. The Chinese of Thailand are extremely close to the Thais and there has been much intermarriage between the races; most of the country's foreign trade, largely conducted from Bangkok, is in their hands. Somewhat surprisingly, the strongly anti-Communist government of the Philippines enjoys good diplomatic relations with China, and the small Chinese minority handle a good proportion of Sino–Philippine trade. In Burma, Chinese traders in Rangoon run what China trade there is. There is two-way border trade with Vietnam, now growing considerably as relations improve. As a general statement, it is roughly correct that the political power in South East Asia rests largely in the hands of the indigenous people: Thais, Burmese, Malays, Indonesians, Filipinos and so forth. The economic strength lies chiefly with the Overseas Chinese, who accept this division of influence, and have come largely to dominate the commercial life of the area, often also exerting indirect political influence. Meanwhile, the Malaysian and Indonesian governments have long embarked on policies to encourage the original inhabitants, respectively the *bumiputra* and *pribumi*, literally 'sons of the soil', to catch up in commerce too: a process largely supported by most local Chinese who recognize that this policy coincides with their long-term interests.

Overseas Chinese businessmen are regarded for their acumen and their integrity remains a byword; it was in this region that the Victorian term 'Word of a Chinaman', i.e. to be trusted, originated. Inevitably, business conditions and practices vary enormously. In Singapore, there is high efficiency and antiseptic dullness, and in Jakarta a creaking infrastructure leads to delays and inefficiency. Throughout most of the region there is official corruption in varying degree. The old-fashioned Chinese approach to trade, where practically no documents are required, such accounts as are kept are calculated on the traditional abacus, where an obligation to family and clan but not to government is the accepted stance, and an official is often not without reason regarded as an interloper, as someone who has to be endured and bribed, still exists. At the other end of the scale, and increasing rapidly, there is the modern, business school jargon-speaking, computerized, air-conditioned, glass-walled corporation with executives as fast and efficient as anywhere in the world. Most businesses of course lie between these two extremes. All do business with China for reasons of sound commercial judgement, patriotism and self-interest, each motive shading indistinguishably into the next.

The fifth-generation Chinese from Surabaya, whose ancestors settled there about the time of Stamford Raffles, the great administrator and scholar who founded the colony of Singapore at the beginning of the nineteenth century, eats Chinese food with Indonesian spices and prefers a spoon and fork to chopsticks, speaks Bahasa Indonesia at work and probably also at home, cannot read Chinese and has never been to China, still feels he is Chinese. So does a second-generation Hokkien in Singapore, who speaks his provincial dialect to his parents at home, has learnt Mandarin which he speaks well, albeit with an accent, reads the Chinese press and encourages his children to learn some Chinese history and classics. Both probably belong to their local clansmen's association, formed from members all originating from the same district in China, mutually supportive both socially and commercially. Some of the old school may still, as shrewd realists in death as in life, hedge their bets and arrange for both Buddhist and Taoist priests, perhaps even on occasion Christian ministers, to attend their ornate and expensive funerals. Overseas Chinese largely stood aloof from much of the post-war civil war in China; regarding events with a mixture of fear and approbation. They were ambivalent to their previous European colonial rulers, who mostly allowed them to flourish commercially without too much interference. They regard their various national governments with emotions ranging from latent distrust to qualified support, usually the former. The degree of discrimination against Chinese varies according to territory: considerable in Indonesia, insidious in Malaysia, practically none in Thailand and Vietnam.

The biggest single political problem awaiting solution in East Asia today is whether or not Taiwan will eventually be reunited with the motherland. Despite the intransigence of both sides, relations across the Taiwan Straits are much better than a generation ago. There are meanwhile still no officially allowed direct commercial relations between Taiwan and mainland China, nor can you fly directly between the two, although a thriving indirect trade has been going for years, principally via middlemen in HongKong. Unwillingness to deal direct stems entirely from the Taiwan side, yet Taiwan-made goods are for sale in Chinese department stores and there are some Taiwan-owned factories in the Special Economic Zones in Fujian province. For many years the only trade was in abuse; punctuated by regular Nationalist calls to counter-attack the mainland and exterminate the Red Bandits which no one ever took seriously, countered by calls to Taiwanese to rid themselves of the Chiang Kai-shek gangster clique. Later, claims to be the legitimate government of all China were abandoned and the Republic of China on Taiwan was just that. More recently attitudes softened further; in 1987 Taiwan's then ruling Nationalist government permitted some direct travel to the mainland. But the official line remains that reunification is out of the question and most Taiwanese do not wish to be incorporated into the People's Republic. They would like to see Taiwan become a truly independent state in its own right, a view which is anathema to Peking. China herself welcomes visitors from Taiwan with open arms and wishes to promote commercial and cultural relations, looking to the day when Taiwan is back in the fold with promises of semi-autonomy on the basis of one country, two systems and preservation of the present social order. There is no sign at all of China abandoning her long expressed aim of reuniting Taiwan with the motherland.

Taiwan's businessmen and manufacturers trade worldwide successfully and efficiently. Despite her diplomatic isolation, Taiwan maintains thriving commercial links with most countries and has built up foreign exchange reserves second only to that of Japan. In some places, the erstwhile embassy and its ambassador and staff now go under another name: thus in London there was until recently the Free Chinese Centre in Regent Street as unofficial representative office, now the Taipei Representative Office and the Majestic Trading Company as adjunct to the commercial section. Often, direct contact with the host government is officially impossible, and any dialogue has to go all the way to Taipei and back again. Most Western governments are extremely careful not to damage relations with China in any way; they are however quite prepared to deal with Taiwan, provided of course the one connection does not harm the other. Everywhere there are various committees and associations formed for the purpose of promoting Taiwan trade which is growing, together with two-way investment.

As what is now called a newly industrializing country (NIC), Taiwan is, along with South Korea, Singapore and HongKong, one of the so-called little dragons of the Far East. Her foreign trade is expanding rapidly and now rates twelfth or thirteenth in world trade rankings, with exports to Europe not much less than those of the People's Republic. It is a free market economy with considerable foreign investment, principally by the Japanese who occupied Taiwan for 50 years up to 1945 and are still much in evidence, and the Americans who rendered massive aid throughout the 1950s and early 1960s. Taiwan is the unsung American success story in the Far East. This began after the Nationalists lost the civil war and retreated to Taiwan; apart from military protection and assistance, phased out over years, the United States also built up the Taiwan economy, improved agriculture and subsidized industry. By the 1970s Taiwan stood on her own feet and rapidly became an economic success. In time there was political development, and Taiwan stands today as a fully fledged democracy. Officialdom seldom interferes in business apart from ensuring that regulations covering any dealing with China are observed. Taiwanese industry is, for the most part, modern and well run and her businessmen are becoming better known in the West as they strive to maintain and improve their homeland's precarious international position. They also regard themselves as citizens of a country that is the chief repository of Chinese culture and tradition and the guardian of the Three Principles of Dr Sun Yat-Sen, the formula for government and people laid down by the '*guofu*/father of the nation' in 1912.

Over the years HongKong has achieved an importance out of all proportion to its size. Its dynamic free enterprise, staggering growth, financial strength, management expertise, clever and versatile businessmen, pragmatic and industrious work force and international reputation have made it a major success story. Now this extraordinary place, which reverted to Chinese rule in 1997 is becoming increasingly involved in the future development of south China, to which it is the key, and is speedily adapting itself accordingly. Over the past 20-odd years two-way trade with China has rocketed. Equally remarkably, this dramatic increase has hardly detracted from HongKong's performance elsewhere in the world. HongKong industry, which began to grow in the early 1950s, has largely moved north over the frontier to the Shenzhen Special Economic Zone, and HongKong itself is increasingly becoming a service centre. The business system is efficient and works faster, and better than just about anywhere else. Communications are excellent, and are now so with China; the banking system is efficient; you can borrow, lose or make money in HongKong faster than anywhere else. Despite the continual pre-occupation with making money, there is now more attention paid to other issues than finance or business, particularly among the younger people who have a far stronger social conscience than that generally obtaining during the 'jungle conditions' of some 40-odd years ago. The grinding poverty and appalling living conditions of much of the work force have very largely been alleviated, in part by a HongKong government resettlement and housing programme which began in the 1950s. Public health and education have also vastly improved, and the various employment laws are strictly enforced.

HongKong has given more support to China's Four Modernizations – the modernization of agriculture, industry, defence and science and technology, announced just before the Open Door policy encouraging foreign trade and investment – than has anywhere else. Nearly all the investment in the Special Economic Zone at Shenzhen over the border is from HongKong. China's annual intake of foreign exchange from the region is huge; Chinese investments in HongKong are likewise. China now accounts for over a quarter of HongKong's total trade, and HongKong itself is the fourteenth largest trading nation in the world. HongKong occupies 0.25 per cent of the land area of China, has 0.5 per cent of her population, and 16.5 per cent of her wealth. Inevitably these comparisons are unfair, as they are so differently based. But the extreme contrast highlights the delicate process of assimilation that is under way. This is not just a drawing of HongKong towards China, but the reverse process too. In the period up to the return of HongKong to China in 1997, official British policy, repeated by the HongKong government, may be summarized as attempting the following, not necessarily in order of priority: to preserve the present *status quo* yet introduce some minimal electoral reform, to not offend China, to achieve a smooth handover, to protect local interests, and to get Britain out of her residual obligations with as little difficulty as possible. Apart from some miscalculations made by the last governor this was largely achieved. Attempts to introduce a largely democratic system of representation in HongKong before the handover were misconstrued by the authorities in Beijing as a possible ruse to prolong British influence and were unsuccessful. The matter was finally settled satisfactorily. China has been generally correct in keeping her side of the bargain after the transfer of power. Recently there have been demonstrations questioning the present system of government, which is of course indirectly controlled by China, but any change is unlikely for some time to come.

HongKong's commercial community is mostly local Cantonese but with a leavening of Shanghainese and an increasing number from the rest of the mainland. The old regional rivalries and animosities have virtually gone. There are also a lot of resident Western businessmen, mostly representatives of international corporations and others from all over the world. There are numerous tycoons, some noted for their flamboyant behaviour and lifestyles, a few for their philanthropy, and all of them devoted to amassing as much wealth as they can as quickly as possible. This has always been so, though now the balance is altering as some of the older British hongs, or trading firms, are acquired by local Chinese interests or decide to move elsewhere, and the day of the old

Western *taipan* is nearly over. The many thousands of Northerners and Shanghainese who arrived over the border in the early 1950s as refugees are entirely assimilated into the community; the younger ones speak Cantonese fluently. It was the Shanghainese who first set up HongKong's textile industry, and despite concerted Cantonese opposition at the time, made inroads into banking and foreign exchange dealing. Shanghainese, it was said, conducted business with more panache than the more cautious Cantonese; aiming higher, rising faster, falling further. Such distinctions have largely disappeared. The Cantonese of HongKong of course find it easy to deal with their fellow Cantonese over the border and up the Pearl River in Canton, for they speak the same language, in more ways than one. Nonetheless it is worth noting that many senior provincial posts in Guangdong are held by non-Cantonese, and Mandarin is of course the official medium of communication. In the past few years many more HongKong Cantonese, like their brethren in South East Asia, have learned Mandarin, so dealing with mainland compatriots has become easier.

Meanwhile, the 'uncles' have been coming. There is a Chinese term, pronounced in Mandarin as *biaoshu*, which loosely translates as 'uncle', meaning not a close relationship but a rather distant relative, perhaps someone coming from afar; it can be slightly derogatory and may even be rendered as 'country bumpkin'. The Cantonese of HongKong used it to describe the increasing flow of visitors from China, not family or friends from neighbouring Guangdong province, but '*ganbu*/cadres' or officials from further afield coming for familiarization, to look at their new real estate, perhaps as part of official missions, or tour groups, or affiliated to the local China directed offices and companies. Since the early 1980s uncles have been evident in the streets of HongKong in increasing number, at first usually grouped together, staring at the tall buildings and neon lights, but now taking all this in their stride. Formerly you could identify them by their China-made Western suits with standard ties, more stockily built, with garlic on their breath, the men sometimes with close-cropped hair, the women drably dressed. Now their dress and manner has become less distinctive and they no longer attract any attention. Cantonese locals regarded them with a mild cynicism, neither hostile nor friendly; after all, their presence is now a *fait accompli*. HongKong people are noted for a sharp, inventive and rather cruel wit. These are the people who also nicknamed a former governor of the colony the boy scout, the Duke of Edinburgh the prince in slippers, and say there are two ways to lose money, one laughing, one crying. When laughing, you do not know you're losing until it is all over; when crying you know all along. They also say that if you do not make money you will come out in a rash and run a temperature.

Before the handover a steady stream of prosperous middle-class professionals, managers, doctors, engineers, lawyers, accountants, architects, emigrated, principally to Canada and Australia, most to stay long enough to acquire citizenship and then return, some for good, reflecting an anxiety over the future of HongKong after 1997. Many who left were themselves refugees, or children of refugees; when it comes to politics and religion, Chinese like to hedge their bets. Lawyers and consultants offering advice on immigration procedures for Canada, Australia, New Zealand and to certain less attractive Third World countries who initially sold citizenship and passports to all corners, did a roaring trade. Few particularly enjoyed their time away, and found it a relief to pick up the earlier HongKong lifestyle along with the new passport. Some may wonder just how useful would be their hard-won passports if there were now a genuine emergency in the region. It meanwhile became fashionable to decry progressive local politicians who had a foreign passport tucked away somewhere. Many HongKong citizens also held a HongKong British passport, a second-class document which did not permit right of abode in the UK and was therefore useless and recognized as such. To get the real thing was infinitely more difficult, and this was largely recognized as a ploy to restrict HongKong immigration into the UK.

Like HongKong, the Portuguese Overseas Territory of Macao over on the other side of the Pearl River Estuary went back to China, but in the year 2000. In practice China had controlled the enclave in all but name ever since 1967; at that time the Cultural Revolution was in full spate, there was rioting and shooting and Portuguese control was threatened. The Portuguese administration sent a delegation to Peking to offer the place back to China, lock, stock and barrel, just like that. This was sternly refused: the Portuguese were not to be let off so lightly. Now the quarter of a million inhabitants, practically all Cantonese, have accepted the future with apparent equanimity. There is a thriving two-way trade, principally with the Special Economic Zone of Zhuhai, just over the border. Macao retains some of its southern European atmosphere in part though this is fast disappearing, and is still famous for its casinos and other delights. All these lucrative activities have continued after the Chinese take-over. Despite efforts by the authorities, it also remains a base for criminal activities such as drug trafficking and smuggling on the part of the Triads. These are secret societies, some dating back to the Ming, whose members are sworn to allegiance and who engage in mystic rites and ceremonies. They also handled a large part of the illegal immigrations into HongKong before the handover.

Nearly all Chinese abroad support their '*zuguo*/ancestral country'. These feelings are reciprocated; China offers backing, support and if possible protection to Chinese wherever they may be within the four seas. Long ago there was no official interest at all but now of course there is plenty. Compatriots from overseas are welcome in China as both their expertise and money are needed. The somewhat condescending air occasionally manifested towards HongKong Chinese before 1984, when agreement was reached on the eventual return of the territory, has just about disappeared. That many of them still speak Mandarin badly or not at all and have a low standard of written Chinese and general knowledge of Chinese customs and history is noted, even though the colonial issue has been solved. There is now frequent envy at the higher standard of living and availability of luxuries and a desire to visit, though things are rapidly levelling out. Gone are the days when some HongKong businessmen were harried and abused as running dogs of the British, a frequent epithet of Cultural Revolution times. Indeed it is now considered rather bad form to recall that this ever happened at all; certainly it is not mentioned. Taiwan compatriots are generally welcome as is their business; both trade and inward investment have grown enormously since it began in the 1980s. Culturally and linguistically they are on a par with their mainland cousins.

The inhabitants of the coastal provinces of Guangdong and Fujian also have a personal connection. Most of the HongKong population has relatives over the border, and each Lunar New Year between one and two million people cross over into Guangdong province on family visits. The Overseas Chinese have links too, though far more remote; many now try to pay at least one visit to the ancestral village. It was remittances from labourers on the rubber estates of the Indies, or railway gangers in California that supported whole villages in the past; nowadays towkays, or bosses, from South East Asia invest or, on occasions, make donations. All Chinese visitors to China bear gifts, this is *de rigueur*, and a frequent topic of conversation among those contemplating a visit to relatives in the old country is the expense. There are still obvious cultural differences, particularly the further inland the visitors go, though distinctions in dress and manner among the younger people are less and less apparent. In the 1970s you could easily pick out a HongKong Chinese visitor on the streets of Canton if only by his haircut, possibly waved with a parting. Now it is not at all easy, though one give-away is still sometimes the footwear; mainland manufactured shoes are often poorly designed, sandals with wobbly heels, or plastic with pointed toes. Some still wear traditional cloth slippers. Overseas Chinese are often on an organized tour and in a sense are treated not unlike Western tourists; loaded on and off buses, guided round scenic spots, shown new industry, lodged in designated hotels. They hear speeches of welcome from local authorities, and an understandable effort is made to welcome them and impress them. A common sight is a party for relatives given by the visitors in an expensive restaurant.

Whether *huaqiao* or *tungbao*, the Overseas Chinese handle a substantial proportion of China's overseas trade and are responsible for much investment. Despite their disparate backgrounds, they all consider themselves Chinese; as the saying goes 'within the four seas, all men are brothers'. They are loyal to China and at the same time almost invariably good citizens of the countries of their adoption.

10
The Long Game: Managing Foreign Ventures in China

The question of whether management in China is different from management in the West continues to preoccupy academics and business people alike. Is China really 'singular and different', they ask, or can Western management techniques be applied just as they would at home? Obviously, if the latter were true, life would be a lot easier. Strategies, organizations and advertising campaigns, often developed globally and at colossal expense, could be rolled out in China with a minimum of additional cost. Adaptation to a new market takes time and costs money. Plenty of people are prepared to convince themselves that what works in Boston will work in Beijing. After all, they argue, basic human motivation is the same everywhere. People go to work because they want to make money, to better themselves, to buy new cars and consumer goods, to send their children to school and so on.

True, we all have broadly similar needs and see work as way of earning money to meet those needs. But above that basic similarity, we have quite different ways of looking at the world. In the 1950s the American psychologist Abraham Maslow developed what he called the 'hierarchy of needs'. According to this theory, people are motivated (to work, to go shopping, etc.) first of all by basic needs for things like food, shelter and personal safety. However, once we have enough food to eat and roofs over our heads, we then start turning to other needs: the need for approval from our peers, for example, or the need for love or for self-esteem, or highest of all in Maslow's hierarchy, the need for 'self-actualization', which means basically the need to grow and develop ourselves as people.

Culture doesn't play much of a role in the lower order needs – people who are hungry or need shelter tend to react in pretty much the same way no matter where they are from – but it has a big impact on the higher order ones. Western people and Chinese people may both seek peer approval, love and even self-actualization, but they will have quite different concepts of what these things are and how to get them. Dip into any of the classics of Chinese literature and you will immediately get a feel for a quite different way of thinking about other people and about society. The respect of other people is much more important and directly tied to self-worth in China than in the West. Family ties are much more powerful, and are replicated in other forms in school classrooms, workplaces and so on, where the teacher or boss is often (temporarily) assigned the role of father. Kinship and the esteem of others are very important values, and continue to be so.

The point of all this is that many Western theorists argue that globalization is leading to greater cultural convergence, and that China will in time become more like the West. Maybe. But looking at the hierarchy of needs concept, it seems possible the opposite could also happen. In other words, as the Chinese become more prosperous and as basic needs for subsistence and shelter are met, won't they start working more to satisfy higher order needs, for self-esteem and love and self-actualization? And if that happens, won't cultural characteristics become even more pronounced, as these things tend to be more influenced by culture? To put it bluntly, will prosperity make China more Chinese? Some would argue that, to counter this, television and other media are diffusing elements of global (i.e. Western) culture everywhere, and this will lead to what the pundits like to call cultural convergence. Again, maybe. But it takes more than a few pop videos and Nike advertisements to overcome 4,000 years of cultural conditioning. And that is as much true of business management as anything else.

Management with Chinese characteristics

Even if we accept that China has a distinctive business culture and that Western firms must accomodate it – then what exactly is Chinese business culture? Most writers on the subject tend to dwell on the 'good' side of that culture. They talk about the importance of relationships and of taking the long view, of Confucian family values and Daoist paired opposites. Strategy is often discussed in quite cerebral terms, with a lot of focus on the maxims of Sunzi (Sun Tzu) and the *Thirty-Six Stratagems* and not much attention paid to the kinds of strategies Chinese firms actually adopt. Many Chinese will argue that the basis of their commercial success has been not Confucian family values, but flexibility, ready access to sources of capital, smart thinking and quick seizure of business opportunites. All these qualities are especially important if China is to compete with the rest of the world.

Others, and this includes many with business experience in China, take a bleaker view. To these writers, Chinese businessmen (and indeed women) are tough and ruthless competitors who are quick to seize an advantage and press it home. Much is made of the supposed 'tricksiness' of Chinese managers and their ability to practise deception in order to fool rivals. It is true that many Chinese will admire the man who is 'eight sides all wide and slippery', that is, clever and resourceful and able to manipulate opponents, but there are rules to the game as well, and there are no more crooks in Chinese business than there are in the West. It is important to make a distinction between legitimate deception or concealment and outright fraud. The latter is comparatively rare; the former is very common.

In the middle 1990s, the Australian academic Geremie Barmé wrote an article entitled 'How to screw foreigners', summarizing Chinese writings in the nineteenth and twentieth centuries on the subject of how to beat foreign competition. It is an interesting article, if not entirely fair to the Chinese, who for most of that time – apart from the years 1949–78 – have been engaged in a tooth-and-nail fight to keep their economy and their markets from being dominated by foreigners. One of the works discussed by Professor Barmé is Li Zongwu's *A Theory of Thickness and Blackness*, published in China in the 1920s. Li argued that business leaders, to be successful, need to cultivate two qualities: thickness, or strong defences against competitors and rivals, and blackness, or strength of purpose and hardness of heart that will lead to ruthless competition and crushing of rivals, especially powerful Western firms that will otherwise come to dominate China.

A Theory of Thickness and Blackness was briefly popular until the Guomindang government, fearing the negative attitude to the West would provoke a backlash among Western traders and governments, banned it. This remains one of the few books on management to have been banned in the country where it was published, and it is now very difficult to find. It is, nonetheless, a valuable comment on Chinese business thinking and strategy.

So which is the true picture of the Chinese businessman: the Confucian paternalist or sage-leader, or the man with the thick skin and the black heart? In fact, both are pretty much true. Many Chinese leaders are skilled at using relationships and networks; some are old-fashioned paternalists, and most, despite what you may read elsewhere, have a strong sense of ethics. The trouble comes when you try to define what is meant by ethics.

Some practices, like feeding false information to competitors, are seen as perfectly acceptable in China, and Chinese managers are quite puzzled when told this is often illegal in the West. Our Western emphasis on 'transparency' is not a concept that goes down well in China, where it is often seen as desirable to keep things as opaque as possible. Meanwhile, under the cover of the smokescreen he has created, the Chinese businessman is quietly preparing and implementing his own strategy. That is not dishonesty, he would say, that is just sound business practice.

The nature of the game

The rules of the game have changed dramatically since Westerners first started doing business in China, but underneath the fluctuating regulatory and economic conditions, there are some basic undercurrents that have changed little, if at all. In particular, there has been the Chinese government's struggle to control the direction and nature of the country's economy in the face of foreign intervention and interference.

For most of the past several centuries, China's attitude to foreign businesses had been ambivalent if not downright hostile. A common feature of both the Qing dynasty and the People's Republic was the view that foreign influence and intrusion into China was a bad thing. Under the empire this was part cultural arrogance and part economic protectionism, but there was also a genuine belief that the West had nothing in particular to offer China. A puzzled Emperor Qianlong, looking at the gifts brought from the West by British ambassador Lord Maccartney in the late eighteenth century, remarked that he could see nothing that anyone in China would want, and doubted that Western manufactured goods would be of any use to the Chinese as the country already provided everything it needed. Western traders were tolerated, so long as they bought Chinese products for export and paid for them with silver and gold, but they tended to be confined to narrow ghettoes like the trading stations at Canton and Macao.

Then came China's long political and economic decline. The Opium Wars broke down the protectionist wall, allowing Westerners to set up self-governing trading stations first at HongKong, then Shanghai and then many other places. Backed, if necessary, by the guns of Western warships, Western traders began forcing their way into the Chinese market. The dark side of this was the opium trade, but legitimate businessmen moved in as well. These men did business very much on their own terms, and generally ran their companies very much as they would have done anywhere else in the world.

Occasionally, there were examples of what could happen when the Chinese government put its mind to supporting its own businessmen. In 1872 the British merchant John Swire, of Butterfield & Swire, established the China Navigation Company to run cargo and passenger steamers up the Yangtse River, one of the great commercial arteries of China (then as now). Swire quickly dominated the river trade on the Yangtse. One far-sighted Chinese realized the consequences if Swire and the British were to take over China's inland trade. This was Li Hongzhang, a mandarin who had risen to prominence following his leading role in crushing the Taiping Rebellion. Li was one of the few senior Chinese officials who understood the Westerners and their methods. With funding from local Chinese businessmen, Li set up a rival company, China Merchants Navigation Company, and then used his court connections to grant the new firm a monopoly on the very lucrative rice carrying trade. By playing the Western game but using the trump card of the authority of the Chinese government, Li had put himself in a position to dominate the market and even push Swire out of business.

Other Western companies involved in river shipping, like Jardine Matheson, tried to fight the new company, but John Swire had come to understand China and knew he could not win a head-to-head contest. So he did what any sensible Chinese businessman would have done; he offered to negotiate. When doing business in China, one later commentator noted, 'common sense, firmness, tact and diplomacy were needed, and the first two of these Mr. Swire possessed in abundance; the last two he could always display should the occasion require it'. Ultimately he struck a deal with Li, giving the latter the largest share of the Yangtse trade but leaving Swire with a very comfortable 38 per cent of the volume (and, incidentally, freezing out Jardine Matheson almost completely).

The moral of this little story is that even when China seems to be weak politically, and economically, its businessmen have a great ability to fight back against foreigners and to work in partnership with the government in order to do so. Li was motivated not by the need to make a profit but by his concern for the fact that Western shippers could, if not challenged, run local shipping firms out of business and impoverish the country still further; but like Swire, he recognized that ultimately partnership was going to be better than conflict. Unfortunately, when Li was promoted to become effective prime minister of China a few years later, he handed over control of the China Merchants Navigation Company to other less competent officials; the company quickly fell apart and the Westerners got their dominance anyway.

Following the 1900 Boxer Rebellion, and even more so after the fall of the empire in 1911, Western (and, by now, Japanese) companies had even more of a free rein. Their national governments had extra-territorial rights over large enclaves in southern and eastern China, and free trade concessions over much of the rest. Chinese companies during this period had little recourse to government backing. In the late 1920s and 1930s the Guomindang government of Chiang Kai-shek, utterly dependent on foreign, especially American, subsidies, was forced to acquiesce to pretty much all the demands of Western traders. Yet even then, powerful interest groups in China could and did compel Western traders to play the game their way. The Ningbo bankers who dominated the Shanghai Bankers Guild, for example, were a strong, united and rich group who could play on equal terms with the Western-owned HongKong-Shanghai Bank – or could until 1935, when Chiang Kai-shek broke the Guild and the Chinese economy almost overnight (see the following chapter for more on this).

Then came the Revolution of 1949, and all the rules changed again. Western concessions in China, apart from HongKong and Macao, were abolished and virtually all Western corporate property was confiscated, although some firms like Swires managed a dignified retreat. The door did not close entirely; unlike the Emperor Qianlong, Mao Zedong recognized that not all of China's needs could be met through internal production, and he therefore allowed limited importation of certain kinds of goods that China needed. This was an extremely limited range, and included glossy art paper for printing English-language propaganda magazines. But as in the days of the Empire, access was strictly controlled and Western merchants did business only with selected intermediaries, nearly always themselves members of the government.

Inside China, too, the system of doing business changed. Late imperial and republican China had had plenty of free enterprise, even though the hand of government regulation was heavy. But in the five years following the revolution, virtually all forms of free enterprise were abolished. Now came the era of large state-owned enterprises, huge factories with names like Shanghai Steel Mill Number One employing 100,000 people and more on a single site. Management rested with a tripartite structure of party officials, union leaders and production managers, all of whom had an equal say in management except that the party leaders were more equal than the others. This too was the era of the 'iron rice bowl', when workers were looked after from the cradle to the grave; housing, health care, child care, education were all provided by the employer, and many even provided meals in workers canteens.

Perhaps not surprisingly, this was a time that some older Chinese look back to with nostalgia; wages were low and working conditions were poor, but there was the certainty of employment and security for one's old age. They feel, like the Yorkshiremen in the Monty Python sketch, that 'We were poor then, but were happy.'

The new management of Chinese industry was focused almost entirely on output. Production targets were the aspirational goal for every manager, team and worker; those who met their targets or exceeded them were rewarded, those who failed to do so languished under a cloud of official disapproval (or worse). Individual workers were reduced to cogs in a machine. Initiative was not only rarely rewarded but was often discouraged. Orders from the top were to be followed unquestioningly; failure to obey smacked of disloyalty not just to the organization, but also to the Party and the People.

There was, of course, a strong flavour of ancient Legalist philosophy about all this (see Chapter 5), but it may come as something of a surprise to learn that the core of the Chinese state production system originated in America, in the methods of scientific management developed by Frederick Winslow Taylor and in Henry Ford's mass production system, both developed between about 1900 and 1910. Working separately, Taylor and Ford had demonstrated how it was possible to increase production by using carefully designed assembly lines where every worker had a defined set of tasks and was encouraged to produce the maximum possible output. Both men were very much admired by the leaders of the Russian Revolution, notably Lenin, who had Taylor's books serialized in *Pravda* and invited senior Ford managers like Charles 'Cast-Iron Charlie' Sorenson to visit Russia and teach the new methods to Russian managers. Scientific management was adopted wholesale by Soviet Russia, ultimately evolving under Stalin into the appalling Stakhanovtsy system where workers in coal mines who failed to make their quotas were sent with their families to Siberian labour camps. Meanwhile, organizations like the Plekhanov Institute were busily disseminating the new methods throughout the Communist world, including China. So when Western, especially American managers, criticize the management of state-run businesses in China, we ought to be careful to remember where that style of management came from, particularly when preaching to the Chinese about how to run their businesses now ...

Back to the main story. As we say, virtually all forms of free enterprise were abolished – but not all. To make up for the inevitable shortages of some necessary goods, the government tolerated and sometimes even encouraged the established so-called 'secret factories', bits of private enterprise outside the state system. In his memoir *Foreign Devil*, the Australian correspondent Richard Hughes recalled a visit to a factory making ball-point pens in Shanghai. On arrival, he noticed a sign over the doorway which read: 'The Shin Factory (Unregistered) For Strongly Made Pens. Forward the Capitalistic Revolution In Aid of Socialism!' He went on to recall the scene inside: 'An asthmatic man in overalls and cap operated a wheel with pedals; two boys were compressing tiny cylinders between rolling pens; a couple of housewives with violet-stained fingers were apparently battering the ends off the completed product with hammers. "Strongly Made" was right.' On inquiring, Hughes learned that the 'factory' was producing over 8,000 pens a month, and that these were being sold all over China by the official state distribution and marketing authorities. Back in Beijing, Vice-Premier Chen Yun told Hughes: '"Secret factories" are generally doing useful work. They can do things which big plants cannot do, or are too busy to do. Some use up waste material which big plants reject. Of course, we can't officially allow them to operate, only secretly. But if any engage in harmful operations of the old sort, we can always intervene' (Hughes, 1972, pp. 159–60).

Letting the flies in

So although capitalism was officially suppressed, it still sometimes lurked in dark corners and the memory of what it was and what it could do had not gone away. Pragmatists like Deng Xiaoping were arguing even while Mao was alive that more capitalism could help to make China more prosperous and solve some of its economic woes, not least the increasingly pressing problem of how to feed a growing population. But no one was arguing for unrestricted and unfettered capitalism – and significantly, very few people who matter in China are prepared to argue that position today.

The decision to allow at least a measure of capitalism to return to China was made with the view that, on balance, the country would benefit. It was inevitable that there would be problems. As Deng himself said, 'If we open the door, we must expect that a few flies will come in.' But it was decided from the beginning that the door would be opened only gradually, and that the government would monitor all developments very closely. 'Capitalist activities' were at first confined to small Special Economic Zones (SEZs). The first of these was set up on the southern island of Hainan. The symbolism of this was lost on no one;

by confining capitalism to an island, the authorities could contain the 'contagion' if things went wrong. Gradually more SEZs were established, including the famous one around the village (as it was then) of Shenzhen next to the border with HongKong.

The SEZs were, quite literally, quarantine zones. Only once it was seen that allowing private enterprise and access for Western companies was not corrupting the Chinese people and threatening the social order were Western businessmen allowed to set up enterprises in other parts of China, and even then there was only a slow and gradual relaxation of restrictions. In fields where China urgently needed foreign investment and technology, like power generation and transmission, the restrictions were removed rather more quickly; in others – significantly, remembering John Swire and Li Hongzhang in the previous century, water transportation – foreign firms were barred from participation for many years. Finance and insurance, areas where Chinese business had even more ground to make up on Western rivals, were also barred to foreign firms until the late 1990s. And sometimes restrictions were loosened and then tightened again, as in the auto industry in the 1990s when it became apparent that China was about to have too many cars for too few roads.

What happened in the 1980s and 1990s was a managed transition from a form of communism to a form of capitalism. The Chinese government and the Communist Party made it clear from the beginning that they would control this transition and guide its course and direction. When the economies of Russia and many of its satellites collapsed following the fall of Gorbachev and the break-up of the Soviet Union, the Chinese authorities felt themselves vindicated. This, they said, is what comes of moving too quickly. Now, although capitalism has to all intents and purposes arrived in China and most Western businesses can do business fairly freely in most places (but note all the qualifiers in this sentence!), the government and the Party remain closely involved with business. At the Sixteenth Party Congress in 2002, then President Jiang Zemin called on business leaders to join the Communist Party and form a partnership between business and the Party for the good of the Chinese people. One of the paradoxes of China is that many of its successful capitalists are also members of the Communist Party.

In the early 1990s, Deng Xiaoping coined the phrase 'socialist market economy'. This was greeted with derision in the West. This was a contradiction in terms, surely: how could a market economy also be socialist? Some conspiracy theorists thought this meant that the Chinese government was only toying with the market economy idea and had no intention of making it work. Others thought the government had recognized the inevitable coming of capitalism and abandonment of socialism and was merely trying to save face. Both were totally wrong. As the speeches at the 2002 Party Congress, not to mention other recent writings and speeches by Jiang Zemin, Zhu Rongji and now the new president Hu Jintao have made clear, the Chinese government is absolutely committed to creating a fusion between socialism and capitalism. The Chinese people may be drifting – some faster than others – away from socialism, but do not bet on that either; around 40 per cent of China's economy is run by so-called township enterprises, community-owned and sometimes community-managed companies not dissimilar to Western cooperatives, and some of these are very smartly run businesses indeed. But regardless of this, the Chinese government and the Communist Party are committed to playing a big role in the Chinese economy for the foreseeable future.

Why? Why not just let capitalism run its course? To answer this question, we need not look very far back in history. A free market and an open economy require open access to markets for foreign companies, and that raises the spectre of foreign domination. Don't forget that for more than half the last millennium, China was occupied, in whole or in part, by foreigners, Mongols, Manchus, Japanese and Western. With the exception of the Manchus, who eventully established a stable government, most of these foreign occupations have seen the condition of China deteriorate markedly, and also saw the deaths of hundreds of millions of people through opium, bullets and bombs. Why, after what the outside world has done to China, should they now believe that we in the West are coming to help them? Sometimes, reading the history of China's relations with the outside world since 1800, it seems astonishing that the Chinese are willing to speak to us at all.

China will do what serves China's interests best, and part of that interest means ensuring that China is economically and politically strong enough to guide its own destiny. And why not? The past two centuries have shown that when China is weak, foreign powers take control and then China suffers. And so China is determined to remain in control. How it will balance this determination with membership of the World Trade Organization and open access to the world remains to be seen; there will inevitably be clashes. But China ought to be strong enough to hold its own. Not long ago an American chewing gum company successfully lobbied the US government, which in turn bullied Singapore into giving up its anti-chewing gum laws, designed to help prevent littering. Reluctantly, Singapore has caved in, and soon

Singaporeans will once more have the dubious pleasure of stepping in wads of other people's discarded gum on the pavement. Singapore had to give in because it is relatively small and weak. It is hard to imagine the government in Beijing giving in to the same kind of pressure.

Getting into the game

So how does a Western company go about diving into this deep and sometimes rather murky pool? These days, getting into China and setting up a business is comparatively easy, at least by the standards of earlier times. It is staying there that is the hard part. As we have noted several times in this book, it is true that there is a lot of money to be made in China. It is also true that making it is very hard indeed.

A lot can depend on the kind of vehicle you choose for entry. Apart from things like agency relationships and licensing agreements, which function in China pretty much as they do elsewhere, there are two main strategies for entering China: the joint venture (JV) and what Chinese law defines as wholly foreign-owned enterprises, or WFOEs.

Joint ventures have had a lot of publicity because, for a long time, they were the only form of Western – or to be strictly accurate, non-Chinese – business participation allowed in China. If you were an American, European or Japanese firm and you wanted to get into the China market, you had to do so by setting up a partnership with a Chinese firm or organization. In this way, it was reasoned, Chinese managers and workers could get quick access to Western technology and managerial know-how. As well as providing immediate prosperity, joint ventures were also a sort of on-the-job training programme for China's managers.

The Chinese government loved joint ventures. Western firms hated them. For a start, only limited assistance was provided in finding suitable partners. Local Party officials might well recommend that the hopeful Westerner talk to such-and-such a man who managed such-and-such a business, but there was a good chance the business would turn out to be owned by the Party official's brother-in-law. The latter might, or might not, be a suitable business partner. Lots of companies, including a lot of big companies, set up with the wrong partner and got badly burned. The orthodox view began to be that joint ventures were too risky and unlikely to make money. Better to go the other route, the WFOE, if at all possible. At this point Western consultancy firms got in on the act and many began strenuously advising their clients to set up WFOEs rather than JVs. These firms produced reports showing that the former were more likely to become profitable, more likely to do so quickly, and had fewer management problems than joint ventures.

That research has since been challenged by academic research suggesting that the opposite may be true, or at least that JVs have as good a chance of profitability as any other type of venture. Ultimately, it depends on whose statistics you believe. It does not do to gloss over the truth here: joint ventures in China are risky, and the majority do fail. But that is not China's fault. The majority of all joint ventures fail, because – and there is a wealth of evidence to confirm this – sooner or later the partners find they cannot trust each other and without trust any joint venture is doomed.

This lack of trust can have different sources. Sometimes it is simply on a personal level; people go into ventures together without getting to know each other, and then discover that they simply cannot work together. More common is the problem of conflict of interest. The partners discover that they want radically different things from the venture, or – worse – they discover that they want exactly the same things, and each is determined to have the biggest slice of the pie. One businessman friend with long experience of joint ventures recommends that Western managers should not look for a company too much like their own. Instead, on the principle that opposites attract, he suggests looking for complementarity: find a partner who has strengths that can complement your own weak areas, but at the same time is weak in areas where you are strong. That way each can balance against and learn from the other, and there is a greater chance that both sides will be happy.

The same businessman also suggests that a Western company can have a perfectly successful joint venture with a Chinese company without taking a majority stake. This again is contrary to orthodox thinking, which urges that 50–50 is the bare minimum and that the Western company should always seek majority ownership of the new venture. Probably in most cases this is true; but the possibility of exceptions exist. If control is an issue, there may be other ways of exerting it than through ownership. The dog in the manger attitude that 'how ever much money the other guy is making, we have to make more' has wrecked not a few joint ventures, and again, not just in China. Even if a Western company holds a majority of the shares in a JV, control is not assured.

Wholly foreign-owned ventures are now approved in almost every area and it is perfectly possible for an international company to set up a subsidiary in China without local participation in the business. But for the Western firm contemplating entry into China – especially if the firm and its managers have limited experience of operating in East Asia – the joint venture can still represent an important and less risky mode of entry. In good joint ventures, knowledge doesn't just flow one way: while the Chinese partner learns about Western technology and management methods, the Western partner learns about Chinese culture and markets. Recognition that each party can have a lot to teach the other is often the first pre-requisite to making a joint venture work.

Joint ventures, often seen as risky, can actually help lay off other kinds of risk. The risk that the partnership will fail can be offset by the advantages that having a local partner will bring. Local knowledge of markets, customer needs and so on can be priceless. Yes, this can also be achieved by hiring local managers and staff; but the benefits of tapping into the collective knowledge of an entire firm are likely to be even greater. And, in event of a dispute with another local company or with some branch of government, if you have a local partner in your business, then you have someone on your side; someone who can speak the language, knows the corridors of power and knows where to apply pressure or ask for favours.

All this applies only if you get the right partner, and that is why partner selection is so essential. The trick is to find a partner who: (a) can be trusted; (b) is prepared to trust you; and (c) can add value to the venture through knowledge of local markets, local contacts and so on. Background research on potential partners is essential, and this must not be simply a matter of studying their accounts (which may be of limited use in any case). Getting to know who the partners are and who they are connected to is of paramount importance.

In 1996 a study of joint ventures in China by the Economist Intelligence Unit suggested that potential partners could be classified into three types, depending on the Western firm's needs and the value the Chinese firm could bring: the 'nuts and bolts' partner, who could help gain access to labour, raw materials, distribution and so on; the 'well-endowed godfather', who could give access to senior levels of government and large Chinese corporations, so speeding up approval for new ventures and so on; and the 'four hands on the wheel' partner, where the Chinese partner is interested in growing and expanding and the two parties have complementary goals and aims. The classification still works pretty well today, though emphasis is slowly switching away from the 'nuts and bolts' partners and to 'four hands on the wheel' types. The first group are very valuable to new entrants to China, but often these partnerships are of short duration. The last group are the kind that can build lasting partnerships and make them profitable.

Other ways of typing and classifying potential partners exist, but the main goal is still the same. A joint venture with the wrong partner will probably end in tears. A joint venture with the right partner can create a business much stronger than either partner could have created on their own.

Employing Chinese workers

Whether the Western company in China is operating a joint venture or wholly foreign-owned venture, at some point it needs to take on Chinese employees and managers. One school of thought says that personnel/human resource issues should be left in the hands of Chinese managers and that Westerners should not get involved, as cultural misunderstandings are bound to result. We think this is wrong. Managers manage people, and to hire people and expect them to perform for you without understanding them is a very dubious practice indeed, on all sorts of levels.

There is a lot of folkore about the behaviour and attitudes of Chinese workers, and rather less hard evidence. Plenty of studies have been done, but many make the elementary mistake of asking workers how they feel about particular issues. The workers nearly always answer by saying not what they really think, but what they think the questioner wants to hear. This is considered polite behaviour, and avoids confrontation or dispute by making the questioner happy. It doesn't, though, yield much in the way of useful results. There is also the problem of distinguishing between deep patterns of cultural behaviour, whose influence is often quite subtle, and the dynamics of a rapidly changing labour market.

One common debate is whether Chinese workers are motivated solely by the desire to earn wages, or whether there are other motivations as well. There is a school of thought among Western managers and consultants in China that to attract the best employees, all you have to do is pay high wages. We discussed in Chapter 2 how wages in China, although theoretically low, tend to rise dramatically if one is looking to attract the best people. And the problem is that anybody can play this game. Our firm might attract key employees by offering them 50 per cent above the going wage; but if they take up the offer, we have to recognize that if someone else comes along and offers another 50 per cent, these same key employees will pack up and go. Top people in China, like top people anywhere, follow the money. The difference is that right now in China they are in a seller's market, and the demand for trained and skilled people, especially managers, outstrips supply. Staff turnover rates of 20 per cent, 30 per cent and more per year are not unknown. The costs of recruiting and training this proportion of a workforce each year is huge, and this can quickly erode the cost advantage of lower wages.

Pre-supposing a Western-style market economy in wages is a risky business, at least at the moment. But for companies prepared to 'think Chinese', there may be ways out of the problem. The Western companies and joint ventures in China with the lowest staff turnover rates, and therefore usually the lowest overall wage and recruitment costs, tend to be those that have adopted at least to some extent Chinese cultural values. Most notably, they put a strong premium on relationships, between staff members and between staff and management. They often try to demonstrate a real commitment, not just to their own staff but to China itself, and show off how their efforts are helping to make Chinese people more prosperous and happy; this enhances the prestige of staff and management, who can feel that they are doing something for their country. Some Western firms have even gone so far as to offer old-fashioned 'iron rice bowl' benefits like subsidized or free housing, education and pensions, things which the average security-conscious Chinese will value highly. All these are ways of demonstrating commitment. This does not work a hundred per cent of the time; the job hoppers will still hop. But as time goes by, a solid core of dependable employees begins to build up.

Leadership is another issue that needs to be addressed. Orthodox Western management thinking is full of phrases like 'democracy' and 'empowerment'. Leaders are encouraged to give people as much responsibility as possible and to become background figures, coordinating and guiding only where necessary. This is contrary to much of Chinese thinking, where the leader is expected to lead. It is his (or her) job to make decisions; that is what they are paid for. Even in Daoism, where leaders are encouraged to use the concept of *wu-wei*, not so much doing things as causing things to be done, the leader still has overall responsibility for creating and enforcing the grand design.

This does not mean that the Chinese like dictatorship; far from it. One of the responsibilities of the leader is to consult with his (or her) people. Good leaders are expected to find out what their people are thinking, and then make decisions that conform with their wishes and needs. Legalism, and Communism, downplayed this step on the grounds that the leaders already knew what the people needed and therefore there was no need to consult anyone apart from a few other members of the ruling hierarchy. But with the relaxation of social as well as economic controls that has accompanied the reform process, we see dialogue beginning to open up again within organizations. There are around a quarter of a million labour disputes in China every year at the moment, and a good proportion of these have as their root cause the failure by management to consult the workers before making a decision.

But – the decision rests with the leader, and once the leader has taken the decision, all are expected to obey it. It is a very serious matter for a worker to challenge or criticize a decision made by his leader, because it causes the latter to lose face. So, once the consultation process is over and the decision is made, it is time to shut your mouth and get on with it. As the saying goes, 'honour the hierarchy first, your vision of the truth second.'

One of the other aspects of leadership that often confuses Western managers is the tendency for employees to regard their managers as public property. Elswhere in East Asia, in places such as Taiwan or Singapore where Chinese business culture dominates, there are legions of stories of workers expecting their managers to solve not only their problems at work but also domestic finances and even act as marriage counsellors. Managers are approached by worried employees at home in the evening, or on the golf course at the weekend. They are expected to respond. This trait, an obvious holdover from the Confucian idea of the organization as a kind of family, may be dying out, but it still persists in many places.

Government: the invisible partner

In some ways, the notion of the wholly foreign-owned venture is a myth. A Western company may own 100 per cent of its Chinese venture, but it never fully controls it. Every foreign firm working in China has an invisible – or sometimes highly visible – partner: the Chinese government.

To repeat what we said above, the Chinese government has no intention of relinquishing control over the Chinese economy. It has divested itself of many state-owned enterprises and will continue to do so, so long as mass unemployment can be avoided. It has stepped back from the day-to-day running of the economy at a micro level. In joining the World Trade Organization, it has accepted most of the tenets of the free market. But government is still there, and it is still scrutinizing the performance of sectors and even individual businesses. And when it feels intervention is called for, then it intervenes.

On a single day in 1996, more than 100 Western–Chinese joint ventures in the city of Tianjin were terminated at the stroke of a pen.

In the eyes of government, they were considered unprofitable or unlikely to succeed, and their licences to trade were revoked. There were more similar closures in and around Beijing in 2002. This is draconian behaviour; what happens more commonly is that administrative and legal roadblocks are thrown in front of companies that are perceived, in official language, not be acting in the best interests of China. In practice the problem may be as simple as the fact that Chinese competitors have lobbied the government to act against them. When a Western company and a Chinese company are competing for the same set of resources, and both need government approval to gain access, then the Chinese company automatically has the initiative. The most famous case example of this was McDonald's, granted a prime site on the edge of Tiananmen Square in Beijing, only to see its ownership of the site revoked and handed over to a HongKong-based property company whose owner was friendly with Deng Xiaoping's daughter. It took four years of costly legal actions for McDonald's to recover the site.

To complicate the issue, China has many different levels of government – national, provincial, city, township and so on – and all have the ability to regulate enterprise to some degree. Often they will have vastly different views on how this regulation should be conducted, and will interpret a piece of legislation or regulation in diametrically opposite ways. Some local governments are more than capable of standing up to Beijing. The municipality of Shanghai, for example, will discreetly ignore many laws from Beijing that it does not wish to enforce. They feel their city is at least as important as Beijing – 'In Shanghai we make the money', they say, 'while in Beijing they spend it' – and have the right to make their own decisions. This works in business's favour, as Shanghai is famously pro-business. The situation changes when you go into the depths of the West, where unreconstructed Communist governments still hold sway at local level; here, even armed with the backing of Beijing, foreign firms can find themselves denied access to virtually everything they need to operate, not only licences but labour, land and electrical power. It is quite possible to complain to Beijing, but do not expect a quick response in every case.

Again, there is no easy way out of this, but history again shows that the companies that have got on best in China are those that have accepted this situation and set out in a pragmatic way to develop a partnership with government. From Butterfield & Swire's negotiations with Li Hongzhang in the 1870s to IBM's long courtship of Beijing in the 1980s and 1990s, there are plenty of examples to show how this works. Accepting that the Chinese government has a point of view, even if it is one with which we do not necessarily agree, is a starting point.

Being prepared to sacrifice some short-term profit in order to make a gesture that demonstrates long-term commitment to China is another. Above all, the one thing that seems to make a difference is a demonstrably true statement – backed up with action – that the foreign company has the interests of China at heart and is prepared to work with the government rather than against it. This doesn't work all the time. But it works a lot more often than beating on the government's door and demanding it be opened. In most cases in China, partnerships and negotiation will beat confrontation and legal action, and that is particularly true when dealing with government.

Thinking forward

Ultimately, the kind of venture that a foreign firm establishes in China must depend on its own goals and what future it sees for the region. There is an often-held belief that Western managers think only of the short-term while Chinese businessmen think more of the long term. In fact, Chinese managers have an ability to think of both the short term and the long term pretty much simultaneously. Newly established Chinese businesses tend to grow quickly and make a profit much more rapidly than their Western counterparts, for example. But at the same time, it is quite true that the Chinese put more emphasis on the future than do Western people. Joint ventures in the West, for example, are often established for a term of two or three years, never more than five. In China, foreign firms are astonished at being asked to commit to 10, 15 or even 20 year terms. For reasons to be found deep in the culture and psychology of the people and the nation – and in the financial structure of their businesses – the Chinese are better at thinking ahead.

The Chinese marketplace is getting more sophisticated, and developing markets to profit takes longer and is more costly. Government, employees and even customers are demanding something more. That 'more' usually takes longer to develop and build up, and that in turn means a longer commitment. There may still be opportunities for quick profits, but by and large the era of the Wild East is over. The Western companies that will make money in China in the future are the ones prepared to stay the distance, learn as much as possible about their new environment, and turn that knowledge into profit. Ultimately, adopting that outlook may be the single most important factor, and whether this done through a wholly foreign-owned venture or a joint venture may become irrelevant.

11

Rushing Into the Future: China's Financial Markets

In the late thirteenth century the Venetian businessman and traveller Marco Polo, one of the first of the multitudes of Westerners who would go to China seeking wealth, observed that the Chinese empire was issuing paper money. When he returned home to Venice in 1295 and related this, we are told, his compatriots laughed at him. This seems a little strange, for Venice was a major financial centre and had itself been using a form of paper money for well over a century. But – and this could almost be a motto when studying China from a Western perspective – things that look the same often turn out to be profoundly different in nature, and so it was here.

The Venetians, like the Florentines and Genoese and virtually everybody else in Western Europe at the time, used paper instruments known as bills of exchange. Rather than carry large amounts of gold and silver from place to place in order to finance business deals, European merchants and bankers evolved a system of credit notes where a depositor could leave a sum of currency with one bank in one city, receive a written note to the effect that this sum was available, and then go to another bank in another city, hand over the note and receive a similar amount of money (less commission, of course; bankers have to make a living) in the currency of that place. It proved to be a good and easy system, and it spread across the Middle East and into India. After a time people simply stopped going through the business of withdrawing currency and began to pay for goods using the bills of exchange themselves, so that the bills began passing as a form of currency. That is how the modern banknote began; as a bill of exchange which could be traded for real currency. The modern English ten-pound note still reads 'I [in this case the Bank of England] promise to pay the bearer the sum of ten pounds', although since the dropping of the gold standard in the twentieth century, anyone showing up the door of the Bank of England and demanding ten pounds in gold or silver will get a rather terse answer.

In China in Marco Polo's day, the situation was different. The paper money he saw was not bills of exchange, but was itself designed as currency; to replace gold and silver, not to represent it. It may seem a subtle distinction, and one with not much relevance to ordinary life, but it is important; in the West paper money was designed to represent or stand in for real money, while in China it was assumed that paper currency would have value in its own right. Maybe it was this latter idea that Polo's Venetian friends found so amusing. Over the centuries, Chinese shopkeepers and peasants have found the idea of paper money rather less amusing. They hated it. It had no symbolic value for them; it was easily destroyed or lost in the fires that swept through Imperial China's flimsy and flammable cities; and most of all the Chinese government itself appeared to have no confidence in it. Soldiers on garrison duty and merchants on contract to the government were paid in paper money, but taxes were always collected in silver.

Under the Manchu dynasty (1644–1912) paper money gradually disappeared, and when Western traders appeared on the scene in force (literally, sometimes) in the nineteenth century, gold and silver were the standard currency, though banknotes had long since passed into general circulation in the West. Chinese bankers were little more than medieval moneylenders, and when the government of China sought loans to help clean up the damage after the disastrous Taiping Rebellion in mid-century, it began turning to foreign banks, notably the English-owned HongKong-Shanghai Banking Corporation (HKSBC, now known simply as HSBC).

The story of the HKSBC is a fascinating one, and needs more space than we can give it here. Founded in HongKong with a branch office in Shanghai, it had at first concentrated on financing Western trade in China, and its fortunes had fluctuated along with the trade. Under the management of Thomas Jackson, who was chief manager from 1876 to 1888 and again from 1892 to 1902, the bank pushed its way into China and became a major player in the fledgling Chinese financial markets. HKSBC became the leading lender to the Chinese government, pushing aside not only other foreign competitors but domestic Chinese banks. Despite its problems, China was still a rich country, the banking opportunities were many, and profits soared. Much of the bank's business was in foreign exchange, and Jackson also had a talent for spotting market trends and knowing where to shift his money; foreign exchange profits were a mainstay of the bank under his management. Many other foreign banks, lacking his skills, went bankrupt or were forced to close, giving Jackson a still greater share of the market.

Jackson regarded the rapid market fluctuations of the Far East as opportunities, not as threats. He was not a gambler; he managed his finances prudently and to strict controls, and the risks he ran were always calculated ones. His contemporaries regarded him as lucky (indeed his nickname was 'Lucky Jackson'), but in fact he was simply a very talented banker. It was he who moved HKSBC's headquarters from London to the Far East, and he it was he who made it into East Asia's leading bank for decades to come.

Jackson's luck, if you can call it that, was to arrive on the scene at a time when few in authority in China had recognized that the country's financial system was out of date. Chinese businesses wishing to raise money had only two options: to make savings out of cashflow, or to borrow directly from the banks, at often very high rates of interest. A lot is said about the 'thrifty' nature of East Asian societies and how businesses, families and individuals are very good at saving; even now, large Chinese companies prefer to fund expansion out of cashflow. This is said to derive from Confucian values. Maybe; but the lack of alternatives in the Chinese economy for many centuries must surely have helped to force those who wished to get ahead to realize that they could only do so by saving. In the West, by contrast, in defiance of the mediaeval church's strictures against usury, complex financial instruments allowing for different kinds of finance existed from 1200 onward, and stock markets were appearing in European cities by 1450. The first stock market in China did not open until 1921 (ironically, the same year that the Chinese Communist Party was founded).

The first modernization

What is perhaps most remarkable, however, is that once the decision to modernize was taken, Chinese banks and businesses learned the Western system very quickly indeed. Prior to the 1911 Revolution banking, like most business in the country, was controlled by guilds, associations of companies who set policy and determined businesses practices for member companies. Three main banking guilds had emerged. One, based in Guangzhou (Canton) helped finance trade in the south of the country, especially with HongKong. A second, in Shansi province, served as main bankers to the Imperial court, at least until the foreign banks like HKSBC arrived on the scene, when the court switched its patronage and the Shansi bankers began to decline. The third was based in the east-central city of Ningbo, near Shanghai. The Ningbo Bankers' Guild claimed ancient origins for itself, with records going back to the treasury bureaux of the Zhou Dynasty in the twelfth century BC, and they were influential in the business affairs of the cities along the lower Yangtze. When Shanghai began to emerge as a commercial centre, the Ningbo banks began to set up branches there, and until the arrival of the Western bankers in the later nineteenth century, they controlled the finances of the Shanghai trade. By 1900 there were over a hundred Ningbo banks with offices in Shanghai. Unsophisticated though their banking methods were, the Ningbo men controlled huge financial resources, and working together through their guild they were a powerful collective force.

The collapse of the empire forced modernization onto the Chinese financial system. In the power vacuum that lasted until Chiang Kai-shek restored order in the mid-1920s, Western banks and businesses made big inroads into China. Chiang Kai-shek's almost total reliance on the USA, especially through his American-educated wife and her brother, T.V. Soong, whom Chiang appointed prime minister, raised the real prospect that, rather as in Russia and parts of Eastern Europe today, the 'almighty dollar' would become the *de facto* currency of the country and that the whole financial structure would fall into foreign hands.

If this was not to happen, then the Chinese financiers would have to learn to compete with the Westerners on equal terms. Led by the Ningbo Guild, they set about learning in a matter of a decade or two a system which had taken more than seven centuries to evolve in the West. Within a few year of the 1911 Revolution, the Ningbo bankers were setting up their own chartered banks and diversifying into broking and share-dealing. One of the leaders of this group was Yu Yajing (Yu Ya-Ching). Born in Ningbo in 1865, Yu moved to Shanghai in 1910 and set up his own bank there. He was one of the first to realize the importance of dealing with the Westerners in order to learn from them. He was one of the co-founders of the Shanghai Stock Exchange in 1921, and also acted as agent or *compradore* for several large Japanese firms in Shanghai. He cultivated relationships with the HongKong-Shanghai bank, and became one of the more important middlemen between the Western and Chinese financial communities.

Yu had long been a supporter of Sun Yat-Sen, and had once employed the latter's brother-in-law, Chiang Kai-shek, as a broker. Thus when Chiang took power, Yu had good connections with the Chinese government. This won him more respect in the Western business community, and in 1927 he became the first Chinese to be elected to Shanghai

Municipal Council, the governing body of the International Settlement there. In March of that year came the abortive communist revolution, during which the communists asked Yu to join their provisional government; he declined.

The end for the Shanghai banking community followed shortly thereafter when Prime Minister T.V. Soong began pressing the bankers guild for loans to support military campaigns against the warlords and the communists. The economic power of the banks proved to be of little avail in the face of a corrupt and despotic government. Yu began to distance himself from Chiang, and grew even closer to the Western bankers as a result. By 1935 the Chinese economy had collapsed; more than half the banks in Ningbo either failed or simply shut their doors, and those of Shanghai followed suit. Yu is last heard of in 1939 as part of a delegation from the Shanghai Municipal Council seeking a loan from the HongKong-Shanghai Bank; it is probable that he died sometime during the Japanese occupation of the city in World War II. The first attempt at modernization had come to end.

After 1949, the remnants of the old capitalist structure were wiped out. Stock exchanges were abolished – the big Shanghai exchange was closed in June 1949, and the Tianjin exchange was finally shut down in 1953 – and virtually all capital was concentrated in the hands of the state. State banks did exist, but their only purpose was to lend money to other state institutions. Once again, China was cut off from the international financial community. Lack of access to foreign capital during the period 1949–79 did not just hamper China's industrial development; it also meant that the Chinese lacked fundamental knowledge about how the outside world did things.

Opening up the Chinese banks

One of the first steps taken after the reform process began was to attempt to modernize the banking and capital markets. But, in a way that was particularly Chinese, this modernization was undertaken as a series of controlled steps. If the Chinese government was not going to relinquish control of the economy, then it particularly was not going to relinquish control of the financial sector.

Somewhat surprisingly, under Mao a number of lending agencies had existed in order to channel state funds to the large state-owned industrial enterprises. These were consolidated into state-owned chartered banks, and four of these banks were authorized to lend money to private enterprise as well. But no restrictions were placed on lending, and the new bank managers had no experience of working in a commercial environment. Many continued happily to lend large sums to the state-owned enterprises (SOEs), with which they already had long-standing relationships. But most of the SOEs were technically insolvent, and there was no chance these loans would ever be recouped. Other banks lent indiscriminately to the private sector. For example, in the late 1980s and early 1990s there was a rush of lending to construction firms building luxury housing. Within a short time there was a glut of luxury housing and a potentially disastrous shortage of new homes for ordinary workers, who needed to be moved out of their crumbling tower blocks and insanitary *hutongs*.

Central government stepped in again, this time giving the chartered banks definite territory beyond which they could not undertake loans. The Agricultural Bank was only supposed to lend money to farmers and food producers, the Construction Bank only to the construction and building industry, and so on. This worked to some extent, but the problem was that there were some sectors needing development that did not have a bank looking after them. However, this was 10 years into the reform process, and the banks and bankers were slowly becoming more savvy. Restrictions on whom banks could lend to were slowly eased. The apron strings connecting the banks to government were gradually untied. Most Chinese banks are still owned by the state – there are now a few private Chinese banks – but they operate largely independently. Indeed, one problem government now faces is to persuade the banks to lend enough money to the teetering state-owned enterprises to keep them running, until such time as they can be gradually wound up or converted into sound businesses. This is a gradual process, for the government prefers to support loss-making enterprises that create employment rather than pay out billions in benefits to unemployed workers, particularly since the latter might well become a focal point for social and even political unrest. This has been the policy for many years now, and is unlikely to change in the near future.

Foreign capital

From the beginning, too, the government knew it could never raise enough money to support rapid economic growth within China. From 1979, the government turned overseas for help. The first to respond to the call were the Overseas Chinese, including those of HongKong, at that point still a colony of Britain, who for long had a major financial influence. During the Republican period, they provided donations to help maintain the government, especially once the war against Japan began. In 1935 it is estimated that one-third of the revenue received by Chiang Kai-shek's government came from voluntary contributions from the Overseas Chinese community (most of the rest was made up of American financial aid). Now, with linguistic and cultural ties giving them an early advantage in the market, the capitalists of HongKong and Singapore in particular saw big opportunities. By 1995 HongKong was investing US$150 billion a year in the People's Republic, outstripping the investments of the USA and Britain, the next largest investors, by more than 10:1. A good proportion of the HongKong money was actually channelled through the colony from Singapore (and some, of course, was channelled from Britain; if British investment flowing through HongKong is counted, then that country's investment in China in the 1990s was more than double that of the USA).

Western banks and other lenders were not far behind. British, American, French, German and Japanese financial institutions all began moving in. The British had an early advantage, thanks to their links with HongKong, and old names like the HongKong-Shanghai Bank reappeared in the cities of China. But the government made clear that it welcomed all foreign capital in whatever form.

Just as with companies moving in and setting up business ventures, however, there were early problems. One of the earliest and biggest was how to repatriate profits. The government forbade the export of the Chinese currency, the *renminbi* or 'people's currency'. (*Renminbi* is the name given to the currency as a whole, while individual units of currency are known as *yuan*; roughly the same relationship as between 'sterling' and the 'pound'. Indeed some Chinese will say 'yuan renminbi' as the British might say 'pounds sterling'.) And as the currency was not convertible, there was nothing one could do with it if one did get it out of the country. So the trick became to persuade partners or the government to exchange renminbi earnings for dollars, pounds or deutschmarks, and this the government was very reluctant to do, as it wanted to build up its foreign exchange reserves. This situation lasted until the mid-1990s, by which time China had the largest foreign currency reserves of any country in the world, more even than Japan, and decided it was safe to allow foreign currency out of the country. So great is the favourable balance of payments today that exports of profits by foreign banks and firms are vastly smaller than the earnings from exports flowing back in.

More serious was the lack of awareness and knowledge of how complex lending markets and instruments worked. This situation has partly been remedied, thanks in part to training programmes at home and overseas which teach Chinese managers the rudiments of corporate finance, foreign exchange and so on. Managers in big Chinese companies, especially joint ventures, are much more likely to understand how these markets work. But managers in small companies remain much more stuck in the past. Like many of their overseas counterparts, they remain sceptical about bank lending and most small firms still prefer to fund expansion out of cashflow. The Asian financial crisis in the late 1990s, when many banks in Southeast Asia over-lent and then crashed, will have left many feeling more sceptical still. In sum, banking and bank lending is still very much a two-tier activity in China; big companies and big banks work together in partnerships which are fundamentally similar to those of the West, while small private companies and township enterprises still treat the banks as moneylender. This culture could take a long time to break down.

The return of the stock markets

In 1986 the Shanghai Trust Investment Company, a subsidiary of the state-owned Industry and Commerce Bank, established a department for trading securities in a single office room on the Nanjing Road in Shanghai. This was the first time that a stock exchange of any kind had existed in China since the closure of the Tianjin exchange in 1953.

As with the banks, from the beginning of the reforms in 1979 the Beijing government realized that a modern capital market was an essential prerequisite to economic reform. Bank lending alone could never be sufficient. As early as the end of 1980, the first experiments were being made with issuing shares and raising money through public offerings of stocks. The first treasury bills were issued by the Ministry of Finance in 1981. The sums involved were small; the first company to launch a full-scale initial placement offer, Shaoban, in 1983 offered just 13 million yuan or about £1 million sterling. At this stage, however, stocks once issued could not be traded; there was no capital market as such.

The 1986 Shanghai experiment was intended to see what would be the impact of trading shares on a very small scale. At the time it was opened, the Shanghai Trust Investment Company's single room exchange was the smallest stock market in the world. But the following year the government set up a larger experiment, this time in the Shenzhen Special Economic Zone near HongKong. Shares in the Shenzhen Development Bank were sold to the public, and a limited exchange was set up so that these could be publicly traded. There followed a tense period of lobbying by the mayor of Shanghai (and later prime minister of China) Zhu Rongji, who finally persuaded Deng Xiaoping to allow the establishment of a stock market in Shanghai. Permission was finally granted, and on 4 December 1990 Zhu presided over the official opening – or perhaps re-opening of the Shanghai Stock Exchange.

A second stock market, at Shenzhen, was opened in the following July. For a time there were strong feelings of optimism. The Shanghai exchange, it was felt, would quickly recover its former glories. Shanghai would gradually displace HongKong as China's financial capital, especially once Britain handed over the colony to Beijing as was scheduled in 1997. Attempts were made to entice both domestic and foreign investors to use the Shanghai exchange. But things did not work out quite as planned. The early years of the Shanghai exchange were marked by a reluctance by traders to use it. No one knew whether its mechanisms would work, or how transparent its dealings would be. Despite bringing in security experts from Singapore, usually regarded as one of the cleanest exchanges in Asia, there were fears about corruption and insider trading. So the government did an adroit *volte-face*; HongKong would retain its pre-eminence as the financial capital of China with a special emphasis on foreign capital. And while HongKong served as window on the world, Shanghai would be used to slowly build up the domestic capital market and would focus on raising capital internally.

That was probably the right move. HongKong was already an international financial centre, second only to Tokyo in prominence in Asia, and its Hang Seng index was one of half a dozen bellwethers of international financial market movements. To scrap it in favour of the untried Shanghai market would have been folly. And, as rapidly became clear, the Chinese government and investors had a lot to learn about running and working in modern stock markets. There were huge technical problems – two paperless share-dealing systems, called STAQ and NET, introduced at considerable expense, had to be closed down in 1998. The predictable problem of insider dealing also emerged. This is not so much a case of deliberate dishonesty as failing to understand the rules; many Chinese businessmen still cannot understand why it is a bad thing. Surely if we can gain information our competitors do not have, they argue, we should be allowed to use it?

Part of the problem too was, and is, regulatory. Driven by the need to keep the capital of Chinese firms in Chinese hands, the authorities have divided shares into two classes. A-shares are shares in Chinese companies which only Chinese investors may own. B-shares are shares in the same companies sold only to foreign investors. B-shares did not go on sale at all until 1992, two years after the Shanghai exchange opened; prior to that time, foreigners could not officially buy shares at all. And to make the playing field still less level, B-shares trade at considerably lower levels than A-shares. On the Shanghai exchange, A-shares command on average 30 per cent of the value of B-shares in the same company; at Shenzhen the proportion is closer to 50 per cent. This might seem to open the door to foreigners buying up large amounts of share capital at a discount, there are limits on the number of B-shares a company can issue and at no time may it issue sufficient B-shares to allow foreigners a controlling interest in the firm.

There are other classifications too. Chinese companies listing on foreign stock exchanges issue shares depending on whether they list on the New York Stock Exchange (N-shares), HongKong (H-shares) or Singapore (S-shares). All these can be purchased by either foreigners or Chinese, but again these trade at values significantly lower than those of A-shares in the same companies. All this makes for a mixture of different categories of ownership, all with different rights and different rates of return on investment.

It is expected that the difference between A- and B-shares in particular will disappear once the *yuan* becomes fully convertible and starts trading on open currency markets. When this will happen is anyone's guess. The government has been talking about this for 10 years, but is no closer to announcing a date. Some Chinese economists think it could come as soon as two or three years time, but others say longer. One thing seems certain; the Chinese government will make the yuan convertible when and only when it feels the currency is strong enough to stand up to the dollar in international trading. The performance of the dollar versus the euro since the launch of the latter will have been watched closely. The euro has survived against the dollar, thanks in part to unexpected weakness in the US economy. China's economy will have to be a lot stronger before the yuan can float, and stay afloat.

Despite all this, the Shanghai and Shenzhen stock markets have expanded rapidly. There are now more than a thousand companies listed on the two markets, including a number of state-owned companies that have sought to use the markets to raise badly needed capital. The financial intermediaries industry has also grown, with more than 30 brokerage houses and hundreds of investment funds established. Most investors are small; with more than 6 trillion yuan locked up domestic savings, the government is eager to get people to dip their hands in their pockets and invest in their own economy. There is still a very high degree of government involvement in the day-to-day running of the stock market, which reassures cautious Chinese investors that their savings are not being gambled away. This, in the government's view, is more important than the free market and transparency that foreign investors might demand. More risky types of investments such as options and futures are not available; at the moment, the Shanghai and Shenzhen stock markets are spot markets only, so that when shares are traded they change hands immediately, as does the money that pays for them. Growth has been slow but successful, and both companies and investors have done rather better through A-shares than any other category.

The pressure to sell B-shares and to get foreign listings remains. Several dozen Chinese companies are now listed on the New York Stock Exchange, and more are clamouring to get in. Yet, research shows that N-shares and H-shares perform worse and raise less capital, and there are also significantly higher costs in listing. Why do Chinese managers persist in seeking these foreign listings? Many explanations have been advanced, but only two seem to make much sense: first, a foreign listing gives the company access to its own supplies of foreign currency without having to go through the banks, and second, it gives prestige to the company's managers. Thanks to their foreign listings they have greater access to foreign travel (and, indeed, to the above-mentioned foreign exchange) and can fancy that they are players in a global game. In that sense, at least, Chinese managers are driven by very similar desires to those of their Western counterparts.

Conclusions

China's financial industry and capital markets are growing rapidly, but are still tiny in comparison to those of similar sized countries in the West, and to their country's own economy. Growth, though, is happening. The Asia crisis and the consequent severe devaluation of the HongKong Stock Exchange has had an interesting impact. It has made the Chinese a little more sceptical about Western-style capital markets, and it has reduced institutional confidence in HongKong. Slowly but surely, the centre of financial gravity is shifting north, away from HongKong and its neighbour Shenzhen to Shanghai. By 2020, at the present rate of progress, Shanghai will have outstripped HongKong in value and volume of shares traded, and will be moving towards the Tokyo level. And it is too late to ask if the big world banks will establish offices in Shanghai; they already have.

That said, China's financial industry, and its managers more generally, have a lot of catching up to do before they will be level with the West. The modernization process that began in the 1920s might have narrowed the gap quite a long way, had it not been choked off during the Maoist era; in 1979, the reformers had to begin almost from scratch. Though it is possible to admire how quickly the Chinese have picked up on the rudiments of the Western financial system, there is still some way to go before they understand it fully and are able to work with it across the whole spectrum of industry. Until that day comes, expect to see capital markets and financial instruments remain simple, banks to remain primary sources of new finance, and government to continue to intervene heavily in the workings of both, guiding institutions and markets towards the outcomes it wants to see.

12
Seek Truth From Facts: Finding Out More About China

It is nowadays easy to get reasonably accurate and reliable information about China, either from Western organizations or the Chinese themselves. Often the information may be somewhat out of date but this is not always so serious as China is in a continuing flux of change. Gone too are the days of excessive Chinese secretiveness, when enquiries could evoke suspicion and giving information to the foreigner could even be deemed treason. For officials to admit a requirement meant there was a deficiency and so in their eyes could imply admitting a weakness. Thus it was only in 1972 that the British team visiting Peking to plan what was then the biggest ever industrial technology exhibition ever held in China asked what sort of exhibits the Chinese would like to see and received the answer: the latest advanced technology that reflects your country's industry. No more could be vouchsafed, and this single sentence was all the guidance ever received.

Like everything else in modern China, all this began to change with the Open Door Policy of 1978. But even now, the Western businessman can occasionally be brought up short by some arcane regulation invoked by bureaucrats. Some of these regulations are themselves secret and not just to the Westerner, but to the Chinese themselves. Or, a report published in the national press may be freely quoted; however, the very same report appearing in the provincial press could be classified as '*neibu*/internal', so may not be used. There is little point in arguing about the illogicality of such cases, and they are now becoming more rare. It is also true to say that it is often not easy to ascertain the facts of a case and what exactly transpired. This is not necessarily due to any obfuscation or unwillingness, rather the general nature of some things Chinese where accountability is sometimes seen through a different prism. So for example, a security guard responsible for the north gate of a factory will deny even indirect responsibility for a break-in at the south gate. Not my job.

In the China of long ago, when the first Treaty Ports were established up and down the coast, it was extremely difficult to get reliable information because of the enormous difficulties posed by distance, accessibility and language. Also, like all pre-modern societies there was little or no centralized local administration with stored information. Such laws as impinged upon foreigners were mostly arbitrary and ancient. For the most part they did not apply anyway, as the Western concessions were outside Chinese jurisdiction, giving rise to the term 'extraterritoriality', or 'extrality' as a buzzword of the time. The huge network of scholar gentry who, until the declining years of empire, ruled China wisely and well, reported through channels to the provincial governor who in turn memorialized the Son of Heaven. There was little lateral communication, and it is interesting to note that this is still an aspect of Chinese bureaucracy to this day. Even now it is hard to find out about a unit or department not directly connected. The people you are dealing with will know nothing about them. If they are to be drawn into a discussion, say for example a joint venture, then the whole thing goes through official channels, and this can take time. There is often little or no published information in such cases to allow an initial appraisal to be made. It is also difficult to find out if you are dealing with the right body anyway. Recently it has become easier to obtain such information; the situation has improved with the advent of a more modern communications system and a far more open approach by some officials.

The rigid centralized system of Foreign Trading Corporations, FTC, imposed by the Communists when they came to power was all-embracing and could not be bypassed. There was little individual contact, and even letters were never signed by individuals but in the name of the corporation. The same applied to the bodies handling insurance, shipping and the Bank of China. This tight bottleneck also meant that buyer or seller, either way, were most unlikely to meet except in special circumstances. It followed, therefore, that it was very difficult indeed to find out anything about Chinese buying, or selling institutions. The one indicator might be a request from the China Council for the Promotion of International Trade, CCPIT, for a seminar covering a specific aspect of technology or industry; it was also possible to glean an idea from questions asked at an exhibition. Since it was not deemed necessary for a Western seller or buyer to deal with or get to know his Chinese counterpart, no industrial or trade directories were published. Officials and managers mostly did not carry visiting cards with address and phone number, so to pursue a contact was virtually impossible. Some relationships, albeit usually both formal and distant, were built up at the twice-yearly Canton Trade Fair, when every six months virtually the same team of Chinese from the Foreign Trade Corporation head offices in Peking would meet virtually the same crowd of foreign businessmen in Canton. But even then it did not go far. A visiting trader might ask after a Chinese official who had not come to the Fair, to be told he was away in North China. Others dealing with a deal under discussion would very likely be referred to as the 'concerned officials', rather than by their names.

By the 1960s, before the advent of the disastrous Cultural Revolution, there was a certain increase in Western promotional activity in China, albeit on a small scale. Technical exhibitions were held in Peking and Shanghai, and one or two Chinese-language journals introducing Western technology emanating from HongKong circulated among end users. The attendance at these exhibitions was organized by the China Council for the Promotion of International Trade which, depending on the subject matter being shown, would invite end users to come from all over China. These same end users would then establish limited direct contact with the foreign exhibitors on their stands, though any subsequent contract or deal was always, and without exception, directly between the seller and the FTC. Further end-user contact would only occur if there was a technical problem, or the user could not understand the instructions for the equipment he had bought. This could happen months afterwards and such an admission was only made with great reluctance. The Chinese-language technical journal circulation was partly handled by the ubiquitous CCPIT, and publishers slowly built up lists of addresses for direct mailing by scanning local newspapers and telephone directories or reading the enquiries received from those not on the mailing list. Many Chinese establishments, industrial, technical, civil engineering, military were listed under a numerical code and in time researchers learned what these codes meant. Thus, for example, 9,000 signified railway engineer troops, and there was another number for airfields, coal mines, brick kilns and so on. This secretive and tightly controlled organizational pattern more or less held good until 1978 and the advent of the Open Door policy.

The rapid influx of foreign business into China and the advent of hitherto unheard of foreign investment placed an enormous strain on this tightly organized infrastructure. It became difficult to know with whom to deal, where authority lay, how one organization was placed *vis-à-vis* another, how the fiscal and banking regulations worked. For a period it was almost as if two systems were working at once; the existing state controlled bottleneck, the new entrepreneurial business springing up. To confuse the issue further, many of the new Chinese enterprises were not true ventures in the usual sense, they were provincial bureaux, or departments, or '*danwey*/units' that had been allowed to use their resources to act independently, so there was not the usual capital formation process. To further add to the difficulties they would usually occupy the same office, use the same phone as before, indeed often share everything with their predecessor. Time and again you would meet an official from a unit; his card would give his name, organization, position, address and phone number, on the reverse side, the same address and phone, but a different organization name, with perhaps the title of president, even, dashingly, a photo. After a few years the situation resolved itself and the confusion abated. But it is still hard to find out what people do exactly, the demarcation of authority, and how one unit relates with another, and will remain so for a long while to come. It should be borne in mind the Chinese often do not know either.

Up-to-date specific information on aspects of China, with notable exceptions, including the military, is now available just about anywhere. Major Western business houses and banks produce glossy brochures full of advice on how to do business, how to get there and what to do when you are there. There are handbooks on China's foreign trade, some Western published, some now China published, worthy, detailed, informative and dull. Usually they are fairly accurate albeit unoriginal, often regurgitating well-known generalities and telling the reader nothing new. Many appear to have been written by the same person. Most guide books include a potted section on Chinese history, culture, language and business conditions. Press coverage of China is far better informed than before and less slanted, either way. This is no longer a sealed country where not even the most basic information is readily published and available.

There are also trade promotion bodies that dispense both information and advice on industry, agriculture, import, export, investment, promotion, technical exchange, training. Chief among these in Europe is the China Britain Business Council in London, with branches in Britain and a network of offices in China. Just about every British firm that is serious about doing business in China is a member. As well as dispensing counsel, the CBBC organizes seminars where you can learn about the China trade, often in collaboration with chambers of commerce. There are receptions held where you meet visiting Chinese delegations, and CBBC led missions to China; you can join one that suits you. There is a pile of background data on file, manuals and a newsletter. The China Association provides a forum for discussion and meetings, as does the 48 Group Club association formed of the first group of 48 British traders who went to Peking to open up trade in 1953. There is a China desk at the Department of Trade and Industry. Academic bodies such as the School of Oriental and African Studies in London until recently regularly ran seminars on China for businessmen. There are other bodies in Britain as well: Chatham House, Asia House, the Centre for International Briefing, Farnham Castle. Similar networks exist, sometimes to a lesser degree, throughout all industrialized nations that do business with China and to a similarly high standard. We have highlighted British sources of information as these are the ones with which we are most familiar, but all the bodies mentioned above have their analogues in the USA and most European countries.

There is of course the Commercial Section of the Chinese Embassy. Certain Chinese official bodies also have separate offices in London and other capital cities: the New China News Agency, the China Travel Service, the China Council for the Promotion of International Trade, China Insurance Co, China Ocean Shipping Co, certain foreign trade corporations, the Bank of China and other major banks. Many large British firms, banks, accountants, consultancies and trading houses are both experienced and usually well informed and frequently offer briefings and seminars. Consulting companies like Ernst & Young, McKinsey and LEK have offices in many cities in China and much experience of working there, and often put much useful information into the public domain. Various specialist journals offer adequate or better coverage of the China scene: examples include the monthly *China-Britain Trade Review* and the quarterlies *China Review* and *China Quarterly*, the last of which is academic. Again this pattern of China coverage is reproduced to more or less a similar degree in the capital cities of all China's major trading partners.

There really is no difficulty in acquiring much of the information you need, again with some exceptions like exact data on sizes of markets, etc. You then have to decide what to do with it. What a businessman should know, or have quick reference to, on his first visit to China falls into the specific and the general. First comes a reasonable grasp of his own specific subject; so much is obvious anywhere. Then follows a general knowledge of the Chinese system and how it works. This is difficult as it keeps changing all the time. The present mixture of old command economy and new enterprise is, as related, confusing. Third, an outline knowledge of China's past, particularly the turmoil of the past 50 years. You must have some idea of what went on, the suffering and the upheaval. Fourth, some general knowledge about China, her size, topography, people. Fifth, advice on how to negotiate, how to deal, such little protocol as will be encountered. These latter skills are best learned on the spot, they can hardly be taught. The visitor will very likely belong to a recognized association dealing with China trade, or at least have received help from his own government who will have given advice on much of all this. It should be made clear that Western businesswomen are equally welcome; a high proportion of Chinese trading officials are themselves women, including ministers and heads of departments.

There is one other subject: a knowledge of the language. Most businessmen have neither the time nor the inclination to learn this difficult language. But for those that are interested, good Chinese language instruction is on offer at universities up and down the country, either for a full-blown three-year BA Hons course, or more practically, short courses by day or evening geared to the businessman. You cannot really learn Chinese while you shave, as the old advertisements used to say; someone has to teach you. It is possible to learn to speak adequate Chinese without being able to write the characters, by relying instead on the official Romanization system; this can be used as a medium for taking notes, but not for communicating with the Chinese, who mostly do not know it. The foreigner can also usually get away with using the wrong tone in speech by context. Usually it is quite obvious what you mean, though there have been hilarious misunderstandings. One of the most famous is '*yan*/salt' which with the tiniest inflection comes out as '*yan*/cigarette'. These limitations will result in adequate Chinese for small talk before a meeting, or asking the way and so forth, not much more. But it will show that you are trying and will almost always elicit polite approbation, indeed sometimes fulsome praise. It will certainly not be enough for serious conversation or business negotiation. For the latter an interpreter is *de rigueur*, if only to check the accuracy of what is said. To make utterly certain, some insist on a second interpreter to check accuracy, but this can discomfit the first interpreter and thus be a two-edged sword.

Depending on how seriously you want to learn about China and the Chinese, there are a mass of books to be read. We will not attempt a suitable reading list for the scholar, but rather choose a few works that will entertain and inform the business traveller who is interested in the people with whom he deals. First, on ancient China, there is Mark Elvin's truly excellent *The Pattern of the Chinese Past*, and also Arthur Waley's *Three Ways of Thought in Ancient China*, covering the very basis of Chinese thought and civilization. Fast forward some 2,000 years to accounts of a decadent empire under Western pressure with *The Great Within* and *Foreign Mud* by Maurice Collis, describing early and later Manchu China under siege and the opium war. An excellent summary of Chinese history from the Ming until now is Jonathan Spence's *The Search for Modern China*, and by the same author are *God's Chinese Son*, an account of the Taiping rebellion of the mid-nineteenth century, and *The Chan's Great Continent*, an account of Western misunderstandings of China over the centuries. Peter Fleming's *The Siege at Peking* is a short, readable and even-handed account of the Boxer Rebellion. Sterling Seagrave's *The Soong Dynasty*, though sometimes historically inaccurate, charts the relationship between Nationalists and Communists in the inter-war years.

Latterly *Red Star over China* is an account of the early Communists by Edgar Snow, and *Stilwell and the American Experience in China* by Barbara Tuchman covers the US and China as allies during World War II. The worldwide best-seller *Wild Swans* is an evocative family history through the turbulent years of Mao, and has spawned a legion of imitators. There is the outstanding *Life and Death in Shanghai*, which describes persecution during the Cultural Revolution. There are also quite a few works summing up modern China such as *Deng* by David Bonavia and *Deng Xiaoping* by Richard Evans, plus numerous works on Mao and his wife; the best probably are *Madame Mao* by Ross Terrill, *Mao Tse tung* by Stuart Schramm, *Mao* by Jonathan Spence and *Mao and the Men Against Him* by Clare Hollingworth.

Lastly there are modern Chinese authors in translation such as *Hibiscus Town* and Bo Yang's *The Ugly Chinaman*. Perhaps the most famous novel of the last century is *The True Story of Ah Q* by Lu Xun, a satire of the 1911 revolution which gives a picture of the end of empire; there is also *Rickshaw Boy* by Lao She, life in 1930s Peking. In the modern period the highly evocative *Metropolis*, by Sun Li and Yu Xiaohui, is an excellent description of China in the throes of massive economic and social change in the late 1980s and early 1990s, and depicts both the opportunities and uncertainties these changes brought. Huo Da's *The Jade King* is a family saga of interest because it is set in one of China's often forgotten minority groups, the Hui (Chinese Muslims).

Films from China in recent years are often well directed and acted depictions of the Chinese scene; gone are the days of ludicrous propaganda. Films such as *The Black Cannon Incident, Raise the Red Lantern* or

Farewell My Concubine have all been shown to considerable acclaim in the West and in China. There is still of course censorship, principally in order to show the People's Republic in a good light. Thus a depiction of the 'bad old days' could be cut, since foreigners might confuse it with present conditions. It may be assumed by the censor that a scene depicting a peasant uprising 500 years ago would be taken as a current situation by Westerners. Occasionally there is also a film with a message, screened at an appropriate time, such as the story of the First Opium War which showed at the time of the handover of HongKong; a TV soap opera of the time also depicted the same events, with Chinese actors dressed up as Royal Navy sailors being knocked over by styrofoam cannon balls. Of course this information can only take you so far in dealing with the Chinese. But an obvious and impartial knowledge of China's history, particularly recent history will not go unnoticed, and will help you build a relationship with those with whom you deal.

Chinese are always pleased when a Westerner evinces a knowledge of their country, their past and their culture. It shows you are interested and have an understanding of what they have been through, and why; perhaps also that you share their optimism about the future. Indeed, this kind of background knowledge about China – its people, its culture, its history, its trials and tribulations – may stand you in better stead than minute knowledge of markets or trading conditions. The latter are constantly changing anyway, and may best be learned on the ground. However much information you can absorb before you get there, it will almost certainly not be enough. Even if you spend years doing business in China, the country and its people will continue to surprise you. China really is 'singular and different', and about the only certainty is that it will remain so.

Bibliography

Allen, G.C. and Donnithorne, Audrey (1954) *Western Enterprise in Far Eastern Economic Development*, London: George Allen & Unwin.

Ambler, Tim and Witzel, Morgen (2000) *Doing Business in China*, London: Routledge.

Backman, Michael and Butler, Charlotte (2002) *Big in Asia: 25 Strategies for Business Success*, Basingstoke: Palgrave Macmillan.

Baker, Hugh D.R. (1979) *Chinese Family and Kinship*, London: Macmillan, now Palgrave Macmillan.

Barmé, Geremie and Jaivin, Linda (1992) *New Ghosts, Old Dreams*, New York: Random House.

Barmé, Geremie and Minford, John (1989) *Seeds of Fire*, Newcastle upon Tyne: Bloodaxe Books.

Birch, Cyril (1967) *An Anthology of Chinese Literature*, Harmondsworth: Penguin.

Blunden, Caroline and Elvin, Mark (1983) *Cultural Atlas of China*, New York: Checkmark Books.

Bonavia, David (1984) *Verdict in Peking*, London: Burnett Books.

Bonavia, David (1989) *Deng*, HongKong: Longman.

Bond, Michael Harris (ed.) (1986) *The Psychology of the Chinese People*, Oxford: Oxford University Press.

Brown, R. Ampalavanar (1996) *Chinese Business Enterprise: Critical Perspectives on Business and Management*, London: Routledge, 4 vols.

Bucknall, Kevin (2002) *Chinese Business Etiquette and Culture*, Raleigh, NC: Boson Books.

Burstein, Daniel, and de Keijzer, Arne (1998) *Big Dragon*, New York: Touchstone.

Chai, Joseph, C.H. (1997) *China: Transition to a Market Economy*, Oxford: Clarendon.

Chang, Jung (1991) *Wild Swans*, London: HarperCollins.

Chen, H. C. (2002) *The Economic Priniciples of Confucius and His School*, New York: Columbia University Press; Bristol: Thoemmes Press.

Chen, Jerome (1961) *Yuan Shih-K'ai*, London: George Allen & Unwin.

Chen Min (1995) *Asian Management Systems*, London: Routledge.

Cheng, Nien (1986) *Life and Death in Shanghai*, London: Grafton Books.

Chi Fulin (2000) *Reform Determines Future of China*, Beijing: Foreign Languages Press.

Child, J. (1994) *Manangement in China During the Age of Reform*, Cambridge: Cambridge University Press.

Chuang-tzu (1964) *Basic Writings*, trans. Burton Watson, New York: Columbia University Press.

Collis, Maurice (1941) *The Great Within*, London: Faber & Faber.

Collis, Maurice (1946) *Foreign Mud*, London: Faber & Faber.

Cottrell, Robert (1993) *The End of Hong Kong*, London: John Murray.

Cradock, Sir Percy (1994) *Experiences of China*, London: John Murray.

Cranmer-Byng, J.L. (1962) *An Embassy to China*, London: Longmans Green.

Creel, H.G. (1954) *Chinese Thought from Confucius to Mao Tse-tung*, London: Eyre & Spottiswoode.
Cronin, Vincent (1961) *The Wise Man from the West*, Glasgow: Fontana.
Elvin, Mark (1973) *The Pattern of the Chinese Past*, Stanford, CA: Stanford University Press.
Evans, Richard (1993) *Deng Xiaoping*, London: Hamish Hamilton.
Fairbank, John King (1964) *Trade and Diplomacy on the China Coast*, Cambridge, MA: Harvard University Press.
Fang, Tony (1998) *Chinese Business Negotiating Style*, Thousand Oaks, CA: Sage Books.
Fathers, Michael and Higgins, Andrew (1989) *Tiananmen*, London: Doubleday.
Fitzgerald, C.P. (1952) *The Birth of Communist China*, London: Cresset.
Fitzgerald, Stephen (1972) *China and the Overseas Chinese*, Cambridge: Cambridge University Press.
Fleming, Peter (1984) *The Siege at Peking*, Oxford: Oxford University Press.
Fung, Yu-lan (1948) *A Short History of Chinese Philosophy*, London: Macmillan, now Palgrave Macmillan.
Gu Hua (1983) *Hibiscus Town*, Beijing: Foreign Languages Press.
Han Feitzu (1964) *Basic Writings*, trans. Burton Watson, New York: Columbia University Press.
Hollingworth, Clare (1985) *Mao and the Men Against Him*, London: Jonathan Cape.
Hook, Brian (ed.) (1982) *The Cambridge Encyclopedia of China*, Cambridge: Cambridge University Press.
Huang Quanyu, Joseph, Leonard and Chen Tong (1997) *Business Decision Making in China*, London: Haworth Press.
Hughes, Richard (1972) *Foreign Devil*, London: Century.
Huo Da (1992) *The Jade King*, Beijing: Panda Press.
Hutchings, Graham (2000) *Modern China*, Harmondsworth: Penguin.
Jenner, W.J.F. (1992) *The Tyranny of History*, Harmondsworth: Penguin.
Jianguang Wang (ed.) (1995) *Westerners Through Chinese Eyes*, Beijing: Foreign Languages Press.
Kealey, Janet (1995) *China Trade Handbook*, London: China–Britain Trade Group.
Lai, Ming (1964) *A History of Chinese Literature*, London: Cassell.
Lao She (1945) *Rickshaw Boy*, New York: Reynal & Hitchcock.
Lattimore, Owen (1962) *Inner Asian Frontiers of China*, Boston: Beacon Press.
Leys, Simon (1977) *The Chairman's New Clothes*, trans. Carol Appleyard and Patrick Goode, London: Allison & Busby.
Leys, Simon (1988) *The Burning Forest*, London: Grafton Books.
Li, Chien-nung (1956) *The Political History of China, 1840–1928*, trans. Ssu-yu Teng and Heremy Ingells, New York: Van Nostrand.
Liang, Zhang, Nathan, Andrew J. and Link, Perry (2001) *The Tiananmen Papers*, London: Little, Brown & Co.
Lieh-tzu (1912) *Taoist Teachings*, trans. Lionel Giles, London: John Murray.
Liu, Binyan (1990) *A Higher Kind of Loyalty*, trans. Zhu Hong, London: Methuen.
Liung, Bing (1914) *Outlines of Chinese History*, Shanghai: Commercial Press.
Loh, Pichon P.Y. (1965) *The Kuomintang Debacle of 1949*, Boston: D.C. Heath & Co.
Lu, Hsun (1956) *The True Story of Ah Q*, vol. 1, *Selected Works of Lu Hsun*, Beijing: Foreign Languages Press.

Lu, Hsun (1967) *A Brief History of Chinese Fiction*, trans. Yang Hsienyi and Gladys Yang, Beijing: Foreign Language Press.

MacFarquhar, Roderick (1983) *The Origins of the Cultural Revolution*, Oxford: Oxford University Press.

Mann, J. (1989) *Beijing Jeep*, New York: Simon & Schuster.

McAleavy, Henry (1968) *Black Flags in Vietnam*, London: George Allen & Unwin.

Miller, Arthur (1984) *Salesman in Beijing*, New York: Viking.

Moise, Edwin E. (1994) *Modern China: A History*, London: Longman, 1994.

Morrison, G.E. (1985) *An Australian in China*, HongKong: Oxford University Press.

Newnham, Richard (1971) *About Chinese*, Harmondsworth: Penguin.

Ng Sek Hong and Warner, Malcolm (1997) *China's Trade Unions and Management*, London: Macmillan, now Palgrave Macmillan.

Polo, Marco (1958) *The Travels of Marco Polo*, trans. and introduction by Ronald Latham, Harmondsworth: Penguin.

Porter, Robin and Robinson, Mandi (1994) *The China Business Guide*, Keele: Keele University/China–Britain Trade Group.

Pye, Lucian W. (1982) *Chinese Commercial Negotiating Style*, Cambridge, MA: Rand.

Pye, Lucian W. (1988) *The Mandarin and the Cadre*, Ann Arbor, MI: University of Michigan Press.

Schneiter, Fred (1992) *Getting Along with the Chinese for Fun and Profit*, HongKong: Asia 2000.

Schram, Stuart (1966) *Mao Tse-tung*, Harmondsworth: Penguin.

Schram, Stuart (1989) *The Thought of Mao Tse-tung*, Cambridge: Contemporary China Institute, and London: SOAS.

Seagrave, Sterling (1996) *The Soong Dynasty*, London: Corgi.

Snow, Edgar (1963) *Red Star over China*, London: Victor Gollancz.

Spence, Jonathan (1982) *The Gate of Heavenly Peace*, London: Faber & Faber.

Spence, Jonathan (1985) *The Memory Palace of Matteo Ricci*, New York: Viking Penguin.

Spence, Jonathan (1990) *The Search for Modern China*, New York: W.W. Norton.

Spence, Jonathan (1996) *God's Chinese Son*, London: HarperCollins.

Spence, Jonathan (1997) *The Chan's Great Continent*, New York: HarperCollins.

Spence, Jonathan (1999) *Mao*, London: Weidenfeld & Nicolson.

Starr, John Bryan (1997) *Understanding China*, New York: Hill and Wang.

Strange, Roger (1998) *Management in China: The Experience of Foreign Businesses*, London: Frank Cass.

Sun Li and Yu Xiaohui (1991) *Metropolis*, Beijing: Panda Press.

Tang, Jie and Ward, Anthony (2002) *The Changing Face of Chinese Management*, London: Routledge.

Teng, Ssu-yu and Fairbank, John K. (1963) *China's Response to the West*, Cambridge, MA: Harvard University Press.

Terrill, Ross (1984) *Madame Mao*, New York: Simon & Schuster.

Terzani, Tiziano (1985) *Behind the Forbidden Door*, HongKong: Asia 2000.

Terzani, Angela (1988) *Chinese Days*, trans. Kirsten Marnano Romano, HongKong: Odyssey.

Thubron, Colin (1987) *Behind the Wall*, New York: Atlantic Monthly Press.

Tuchman, Barbara W. (1971) *Stilwell and the American Experience in China*, London: Macmillan, now Palgrave Macmillan.

Varè, Daniel (1954) *Novels of Yen-ching*, London: Methuen.
Waley, Arthur (1934) *The Way and Its Power*, London: George Allen & Unwin.
Waley, Arthur (1939) *Three Ways of Thought in Ancient China*, London: George Allen & Unwin.
Waley, Arthur (1946) *Chinese Poems*, London: Unwin.
Warner, Malcolm (1992) *How Chinese Managers Learn*, London: Macmillan, now Palgrave Macmillan.
Welsh, Frank (1993) *A History of HongKong*, London: HarperCollins.
White, Theodore H. (1978) *In Search of History*, New York: Warner Books.
Wilson, Dick (1996) *China: The Big Tiger*, London: Little, Brown & Co.
Wood, Frances (1998) *No Dogs and Not Many Chinese*, London: John Murray.
Wright, Mary Clabaugh (1957) *The Last Stand of Chinese Conservatism*, Stanford, CA: Stanford University Press.
Yang, Bo (1992) *The Ugly Chinaman*, trans. Don J. Cohn and Jing Qing, St Leonards, NSW: Allen & Unwin.

Index